The Peshtigo Fire of 1871

A Captivating Guide to the Deadliest Wildfire in the History of the United States of America That Occurred in Northeastern Wisconsin

© Copyright 2020

All Rights Reserved. No part of this book may be reproduced in any form without permission in writing from the author. Reviewers may quote brief passages in reviews.

Disclaimer: No part of this publication may be reproduced or transmitted in any form or by any means, mechanical or electronic, including photocopying or recording, or by any information storage and retrieval system, or transmitted by email without permission in writing from the publisher.

While all attempts have been made to verify the information provided in this publication, neither the author nor the publisher assumes any responsibility for errors, omissions or contrary interpretations of the subject matter herein.

This book is for entertainment purposes only. The views expressed are those of the author alone, and should not be taken as expert instruction or commands. The reader is responsible for his or her own actions.

Adherence to all applicable laws and regulations, including international, federal, state and local laws governing professional licensing, business practices, advertising and all other aspects of doing business in the US, Canada, UK or any other jurisdiction is the sole responsibility of the purchaser or reader.

Neither the author nor the publisher assumes any responsibility or liability whatsoever on the behalf of the purchaser or reader of these materials. Any perceived slight of any individual or organization is purely unintentional.

Free Bonus from Captivating History (Available for a Limited time)

Hi History Lovers!

Now you have a chance to join our exclusive history list so you can get your first history ebook for free as well as discounts and a potential to get more history books for free! Simply visit the link below to join.

Captivatinghistory.com/ebook

Also, make sure to follow us on Facebook, Twitter and Youtube by searching for Captivating History.

Contents

FREE BONUS FROM CAPTIVATING HISTORY (AVAILABLE FOR A LIMITED TIME) 5
INTRODUCTION 1
CHAPTER 1 - BEFORE THE BLAZE 3
CHAPTER 2 - LIFE IN PESHTIGO 11
CHAPTER 3 - ASH LIKE SNOW 17
CHAPTER 4 - NATURE LIFTED UP ITS VOICE 26
CHAPTER 5 - A HOLOCAUST OF FIRE 34
CHAPTER 6 - AMONG THE ASHES 45
CHAPTER 7 - FLICKERS OF HOPE 56
CHAPTER 8 - COMPOSED OF WIND AND FIRE 67
CHAPTER 9 - WILDFIRES THROUGH AMERICAN HISTORY 75
CONCLUSION 87
SOURCES 89

Once in water up to our necks, I thought we would, at least be safe from fire, but it was not so; the flames darted over the river as they did over land, the air was full of them, or rather the air itself was on fire.

- Father Peter Pernin

Introduction

It's likely true that most people picking up this book have never even heard of a place called Peshtigo. This is hardly surprising: this little town on the shores of Lake Michigan is hardly a remarkable place in the modern day. Its residents number less than four thousand, and there's nothing particularly special about it at first glance.

But one does have to look twice at its motto. "A city rebuilt from the ashes."

Peshtigo may be just another small Wisconsin town today, but a hundred and fifty years ago, it really was nothing but ashes. This town was one of the hardest hit in the deadliest wildfire event in American history—and no, I'm not talking about the Great Chicago Fire, even though it also occurred on the very same night. The Great Peshtigo Fire of 1871 claimed four times as many lives as the fire in Chicago, and yet this cruel twist of fate has left it almost unheard-of, while the (untrue) tale of Catherine O'Leary's cow continues to echo through the centuries with unabated vigor.

The story of the Great Peshtigo Fire has not been told nearly often enough, and yet it is a story that will captivate every reader. Parts of it seem to border on science fiction: trees exploding in the heat of the fire, a tornado made of flames sweeping through an entire town in a single hour, birds caught up and burned in mid-air. Yet all of it is true, and so are the stories of the people who witnessed the fire first-hand and survived it.

Read on to discover the stories of the courageous men, women, and even children who somehow faced America's deadliest fire and lived to tell their mesmerizing stories. Run alongside five-year-old Amelia Desrochers as she fled from the horde of advancing flames. Spend six hours in the frigid Peshtigo River with Father Peter Pernin as he watched the sky turn to fire above his head. Feel the desperation of Lars Korstad as he fought to save his wife and nine-day-old daughter. And hide in a dark well with teenager Joseph LaCrosse, trying his best to save a baby girl from the most horrific of fates.

This is not just the story of some big fire. This is a story of hope, sacrifice, and survival.

Chapter 1 – Before the Blaze

Illustration I: A member of the Ojibwe tribe, photographed in 1913

The small town of Peshtigo, Wisconsin, boasting a population of fewer than four thousand people, rests on the banks of the breathtaking Lake Michigan, not far from the more well-known city of Green Bay. Today, Peshtigo is best known for the fire that almost destroyed it. But this tenacious little town has centuries of history behind it, starting long before the blaze began.

The oldest evidence that archaeology has been able to unearth of humans living in modern-day Wisconsin dates back thousands of years. Once, the green forests and serene lakes of the Badger State were all hidden beneath a tremendous layer of permafrost. Instead of endless woods, Wisconsin was a tundra, its subsoil permanently frozen. Gigantic creatures roamed an icy wasteland: beavers that stood eight feet high, twenty-foot-long sloths weighing four tons, muskoxen with spreading horns, and enormous mastodons. The latter looked a little like elephants, except they weighed nearly two tons heavier and had tusks that were eight feet long.

But even these giants were not invincible. The Boaz mastodon, a fossil discovered in 1897 by children playing in a quarry, is evidence of that. The ten-foot-tall creature—whose bones now rest in a Wisconsin museum—may have been killed by human hunters, judging by the fluted quartzite spearhead that was found alongside it. Paleo-Indians, the first human inhabitants of the modern-day United States, may have crossed the Bering Strait when it was still frozen solid during the Ice Age. About 9,000 years ago, they lived on Wisconsin's tundra, acting as nomadic hunter-gatherers that moved wherever their huge prey went. It's uncertain whether they were actually able to hunt these gigantic animals or if they simply scavenged on their carcasses, but numerous archaeological sites have been found where these ancient peoples processed tons upon tons of meat.

For thousands of years, the Paleo-Indians lived their simple lifestyle, traveling across the frozen face of Wisconsin in pursuit of animals the size of buildings. Their diet largely consisted of meat, as plant life was rare in this frozen wilderness. But the world began to change. It started to thaw, and green things grew, and the enormous creatures that the Paleo-Indians lived on eventually died out. A new era arrived: the Archaic Period.

Starting around 4000 BCE, the Archaic Period saw people having to change their ways as they struggled to survive in a very different world. Great conifer forests had grown up as the tundra receded, revealing the lakes that we know today.

The ground, which had been frozen solid for millennia, had also thawed, exposing natural treasures hidden deep in the soil. Ancient Wisconsin, like many other places all over the United States, was extremely rich in copper. But unlike the other states, Wisconsin's copper wasn't present as copper oxide or other copper compounds; instead, the pure copper metal was prevalent in many different sites and easily accessible, even with rudimentary methods of mining. The people that rose up in this area thus became known as the Copper Culture.

The people of the Copper Culture populated much of the Great Lakes area, including Wisconsin, and they were truly ahead of their time. They learned how to heat the copper to make it more malleable, hammering and folding it into a variety of shapes and creating all kinds of objects. Some of these, especially in the Early Archaic Period, were purely utilitarian: arrowheads, fishhooks, harpoons, and even woodworking tools. But as time wore on, and as peace and stability brought prosperity to the Copper Culture, the people began to turn their hands to making gentler things. Bracelets and ornaments were created around 2000 BCE, and the Copper Culture were also some of the first Native Americans to practice ritual burial.

In the Woodland Period, starting around 1000 BCE, the Havana Hopewell Culture took the concept of ritual burial a step further.

Arriving in the Wisconsin area, the Hopewellians were faced with a world that looked very different than the prey-rich tundra where the Paleo-Indians had lived. Now, Wisconsin had become utterly covered in forests. Prey was kept in balance thanks to an abundance of natural predators, and people turned more and more to plant life for food instead of eating the meaty diet of those who had gone before. For the first time, the Wisconsin soil was tilled and planted, and the Hopewellians began to grow crops.

These people also did some hunting, but their staple diet consisted of corn. Cornfields were planted all around their little villages. These people were not nomadic in the least. They were people of the earth, and they left their mark where they had lived by building great burial mounds for their dead.

Burial mounds are not the only legacy of these ancient people, though. Some of the mounds that they built are much more mysterious.

The 1st millennium BCE saw the construction of some of the United States' most famous historical landmarks: the great effigy mounds. These huge constructions of heaped earth would be feats of engineering even today, let alone three thousand years ago. It's unclear how exactly they were built or why. Today, three thousand of them remain, although there may have been as many as twenty thousand of these mysterious constructions. Most of them are burial sites, possibly for important or high-ranking people in Hopewellian society. They are made in the image of all kinds of animals, such as bear, deer, rabbits, and birds, and sometimes that of people, like the Man Mound near Baraboo, Wisconsin. It's thought that these animals and people represent spirits that were important in the Hopewellian religion, but their real origins remain shrouded in mystery. This millennia-old legacy of the Hopewellians endures to this day; its meaning, so far, does not.

Earth mounds continued to be important for later peoples, too. Arriving in Wisconsin around 1050 CE as they expanded upriver, Mississippian peoples had more practical uses for the buildings they created out of the earth. These peoples established a settlement at modern-day Aztalan in the south of Wisconsin, where they hunted some animals but mostly farmed. Vast fields of corn spread out in every direction from their settlement, where they lived in wigwams, but they also built large earthen enclosures that can still be seen to this day. These earthen walls were likely used to keep enemies at bay, although their exact purpose is uncertain.

Generations of native peoples had lived in what is now the United States for thousands of years when the first Europeans began to arrive. The first European to lay eyes on Wisconsin was a remarkable young man named Jean Nicolet. He was a young man whose approach to those native peoples was unique in that it was wholeheartedly peaceful.

* * * *

Jean was born in Normandy, France, in 1598 to a royal mailman and his wife. The 17th century was an era of great colonial expansion. It was during Jean's lifetime that the *Mayflower* set sail, and while the British focused on building Plymouth Colony, the French had occupied Canada since 1534, and they were trying to figure out how to fit their agendas in with the reality that Native Americans had already made their homes in the land that the French hoped to claim.

Jean was still a young man when he knew that what he wanted most was to see the New World with his own eyes. He was a pleasant, easy-going young person with a gift for languages that would stand him in good stead in later life. It wasn't hard for him to gain passage to Canada on a ship, and he moved to the New World more or less permanently in 1619 at the age of 22.

He was 35 when he was sent on his most famous expedition. Given a canoe and some provisions, Jean was sent where no European had ever gone before: along the Great Lakes. Accompanied by seven guides from the Huron area, he paddled from one mighty lake to another, and while none can envy him the dangers that he must have faced—from wild animals to uncharted waters—he must have been privy to an absolutely breathtaking view of American nature untouched by pollution. Wisconsin was in the depth of summer when he arrived, and the lakes were as still as glass and as mighty as the seas; the rising trees surrounded him, woods that were hundreds of years old and filled with splendid animals—and wary people.

The peoples who inhabited the Wisconsin area at the time included the Ho-Chunk and the Menominee. They had never seen a white-skinned person before, much less one dressed with the extravagance of an honored explorer. Jean's colorful clothes confused them, and so did the long metal thing he carried by his side, an object that could spit death at any second. Tragically, armed Europeans were a sight that the Native Americans would become all too familiar with in the years that followed.

But for the Ho-Chunk, it was good news because Jean wasn't like the other explorers. The greed and arrogance of Columbus was something that he didn't bring with him in his first expedition to Wisconsin. Indeed, Jean may have gotten along better with native people than with his own. Shortly after his arrival in Canada in 1619, Jean had moved in with the Nipissing people of Lake Huron, befriending them to such an extent that he was even involved in their councils. Jean wasn't a colonist. He was a diplomat.

Thanks to his command of the Nipissing language, Jean was able to communicate to some extent with the Ho-Chunk, and it wasn't long before he was firm friends with them too. He continued to travel around the Wisconsin area, heading farther and farther north and meeting up with the Ho-Chunk near Green Bay (not far at all from the place where Peshtigo would be built), which would eventually become one of the first European settlements in Wisconsin. There, far from causing war and strife, Jean actually mediated between the Ho-Chunk and a neighboring tribe, bringing an end to a conflict that had claimed many lives between them. He was hailed as a friend and a peacemaker, and when winter came, Jean spent it happily with the Ho-Chunk as if he was one of their own people.

For nearly a hundred years after Jean's arrival, the French continued to more or less follow his example of peace and diplomacy with the natives. In 1685, Fort St. Nicholas was established, and the French began to actively trade with the natives as they established a bustling trade in the furs of animals like mink and ermine. By the beginning of the 18th century, the French had established themselves firmly in the area alongside the Native Americans, even importing slaves from Africa.

The peace did not last long, though. Sadly, French-Native American relations eventually went the way that most relationships between Europeans and Native Americans did. In 1728, open war was declared with another tribe, the Fox Indians, and the bloody conflict continued until two-thirds of the Fox were dead, and they were forced to leave the area.

Thirty years later, the land that the French had fought so hard for was snatched away from them when the British took control of Wisconsin. During British occupation, more and more Europeans began to settle around the area of what would become Peshtigo, less than fifty miles from Green Bay itself. The area had been well explored by the French fur traders by the time the British first arrived. However, the British were less interested in fur and more interested in mining; in the 19th century, many of them only came to the area temporarily, and instead of building homes, they simply burrowed into the hillsides near their mines—hence the term "Badger State" later becoming the nickname of Wisconsin.

The British held Wisconsin for only twenty years before the American Revolution threw off the shackles of the Old World and landed the state firmly in the grasp of the American colonists with the signing of the Treaty of Paris in 1783. It became the 30th state in 1848, but long before Wisconsin became a state, Americans began to expand farther and farther into its vast wilderness.

Two such Americans were David Jones and Erastus Bailey. Arriving on the shores of Lake Michigan in 1838, the two men saw the tremendous potential in Wisconsin's forests. They decided that a sawmill would be hugely useful in the area—and they were right. Their sawmill was soon extremely busy as the trade in lumber bloomed in the area, feeding the voracious appetite of an expanding US that needed timber to build homes for a booming population. In only a few years, a little town had sprung up around the sawmill.

It was given a Native American name, Peshtigo. Depending on the dialect, it could mean "snapping turtle," "wild goose river," or "rapids." Whatever the meaning of the town's name, its people were peaceful and prosperous, working hard at the exciting frontier life they led—and utterly unaware of the terrible disaster that would strike them.

Chapter 2 – Life in Peshtigo

The Great Fire of Peshtigo is one of those historical events that can feel almost surreal to read about. There is so much about this blaze that's almost incomprehensible: the sheer scale of it, the speed with which it devastated so many lives. But this piece of history is very real indeed, and it involved real, ordinary people seeking better lives in a booming American frontier town.

The late 19th century had brought something close to stability to the United States after a century of turmoil, starting with the American Revolution and only settling down after the devastating and bloody conflict of the American Civil War. Once the war was over, Americans began to set their eyes on the frontiers of their enormous and largely unexplored country. While hundreds of them famously made their way west, others headed to the north instead. The great period of American expansion had begun.

Wisconsin was no exception. It was a paradise of natural resources, not only for Americans but also for the floods of immigrants from the overcrowded Old World. With its lead-rich hills, fertile lands, and great forests of useful trees, Wisconsin attracted thousands of people. In fact, the state was home to around one million people by the end of the 19th century. The construction of a railroad into the state became a lifeline to its economy, and business began to boom.

Many of these businesses were, at first, farms. These were sold in parcels of eighty acres at $1.25 an acre, meaning that impoverished families could buy a useful-sized piece of land for the equivalent of around $2,000 in the modern day. There was a downside, though: these lands were completely wild. They hadn't felt the bite of a plow since the time of the Mississippians almost a thousand years before, and great woods had grown up where cornfields once stood, making it almost impossible to farm there. The ground was fertile, though, and these families were determined to find a way to survive. Even though it could take a decade for a small family to clear an average-sized farm, they chipped away at it with a good will, knowing that they had to do it to survive.

One family that was willing to tackle almost anything in order to survive was the Desrochers family. The Desrochers lived in typical primitive pioneer conditions. Their single-roomed shack made *Little House on the Prairie* look like a five-star hotel in comparison. It had just one window, and there was barely enough space for the two parents and five children. Among them was a little girl named Amelia. Only five years old, Amelia was too young to be a real part of the tremendous struggle that her family was going through in order to establish themselves as farmers, but that struggle was evident as setback after setback struck them. Most recently, Amelia's father, Charles, had fallen ill. Since he was bedridden, he was unable to work and feed his family, and worry mounted as the days ticked by. Farming has never been an easy job, but farming in those days was almost too difficult to even imagine.

To make farming families' lives even harder in Wisconsin, one of its most important crops had been almost completely wiped out during the Civil War. Chinch bugs—tiny gray and white beetles that feed on plants—had attacked the wheat crops during that time, causing absolute devastation to what had been one of the most important crops in the area. Desperate to survive, the farmers had little choice but to convert their wheat fields into grazing lands instead and find an animal that could thrive there. That animal proved to be the dairy cow.

By the 1870s, dairy farming proved to be the most common agricultural enterprise all over the state. Peshtigo families had often kept a cow or two—almost all of the farms were self-sufficient to an extent, and a house cow was an integral part of feeding the family—but now cheese and butter became some of Wisconsin's most important exports. Around 90 percent of farms owned dairy cows. As it turned out, this would prove to be a good thing (a lifesaving thing, even) for the Villers family, and they didn't even farm in Peshtigo.

It's not clear why the Villers had come to Peshtigo during that fateful October of 1871. They lived elsewhere in Wisconsin, so it is possible they had come to stay with relatives. At any rate, they were staying in a house in Peshtigo that day. Martin and Octavia Villers were the parents of a beautiful little baby girl named Florence. They had also adopted an orphan boy. Illness and accidents claimed hundreds of people out on the frontier, and fourteen-year-old Joseph LaCrosse's parents were among those who were not so lucky. Many frontier orphans had to fend for themselves. Joseph had been fortunate to be taken in by the Villers, and he seemed to know it, treating them with the deepest gratitude and forming a powerful bond with the infant Florence.

Not all of the residents of Peshtigo were farmers, though. Bailey and Jones had suspected, when they built their sawmill in 1838, that the area was promising for the lumber industry, and they were right. 19th-century America had an insatiable appetite for wood: homes, railroads, wagons, paper—they all needed trees. Americans were processing the great woods of Wisconsin faster than lumberjacks could tear them down. In an era without chainsaws or trucks, trees had to be cut down by hand with saws and axes, a laborious process involving huge numbers of people. Accordingly, people from all walks of life flocked to Peshtigo to work in the logging industry.

One such mill worker was Lars Korstad, who had come a very long way to work in Peshtigo. Born in Norway, Lars left an overcrowded Old World behind to seek his fortune in greener pastures, and those pastures turned out to be Wisconsin. Arriving in 1864, Lars had barely a penny to his name. In fact, he was so poor that he could only pay passage across the sea for one person, meaning that his beloved wife had to be left behind in Norway. He left her with the promise that he would work hard and earn enough money to bring her to America too—a promise that he kept. It took him three years of backbreaking work as a millwright in Peshtigo, but he did it. In 1867, Mrs. Korstad joined him.

The Korstads lived in a tiny shanty that was even poorer than the Desrochers' shack. There was no money for a real wooden floor; instead, they simply covered the dirt with sawdust in a bid to keep the cold and wet out. Their bedding, too, consisted of sacks filled with sawdust. There was no electricity in this rural area, and it must have been shockingly primitive for Mrs. Korstad. Still, at least they were together.

It was in this hopeless little shelter that Mrs. Korstad brought forth their first child. Lars was at work the night of September 30th, 1871, when Mrs. Korstad felt the first pangs of labor come upon her; she was utterly alone in her tiny, dirty home when she gave birth to a baby girl. When Lars got home, he found that his wife was cradling his tiny daughter in her arms, having valiantly delivered her without help. They named the child Anna, which means "grace."

The Korstads were only a single example of the immigrants who came to Wisconsin, considering even that primitive life to be far better than what they had left behind. They came from all over the Old World, including Germany, Scandinavia, Ireland, England, and Italy, to name just a few. Walking down the main street of Peshtigo, one could hear all kinds of different accents in just a few minutes. But the diversity did not run as far as skin color. The vast majority of the immigrants who came to Wisconsin were Caucasian; only about 10 percent of Peshtigo's population was of African descent. The rest were made up of whites and what was left of the Native Americans. These were the Ojibwe, which means "puckered up," a reference to the puckered seams of the moccasins they wore. This was the name that other tribes called them, though. The Ojibwe tribe actually called themselves "Anishinaabe," "True People."

First contacted around 1615 when French explorer Samuel de Champlain—the governor under whom Jean Nicolet served—reached the Lake Huron area, the Ojibwe originally had excellent relations with the Europeans. Siding with the French and engaging in successful trade with them, their greatest enemies during the 17th century proved to be fellow natives, mainly the Iroquois. The Iroquois were conquered in 1701, and the Ojibwe lived peacefully for more than a century alongside the French and later the British. There was a small revolt against the British in the mid-18th century, but the Ojibwe of Wisconsin kept out of it, and, on the whole, they were fairly content with their new neighbors.

Everything changed when the Americans got involved. Around the same time as Peshtigo was being built, American expansionists began to demand that the natives get out of their way. Struggling during a war with the Dakota tribe, the Ojibwe didn't have the manpower to fight the Americans, and they were forced to cede the vast majority of their lands to white Americans during the 1840s. Even this was not enough. The Ojibwe were in danger of having all their Wisconsin lands taken from them, and they could only manage to cling to a small area by giving up the lands they still held in Minnesota.

By 1871, the Ojibwe were confined to tiny reservations, which consisted of infertile land that was no good at all for farming. They were forced to sell even these lands to the lumber industry in order to survive and became little more than slaves working for the lumber companies themselves.

It's understandable then that tension between the white and Ojibwe residents of Peshtigo ran very high. Whites still distrusted the "savages" and saw them as inferior; the Ojibwe were abundantly aware that the Americans had taken their entire way of life and most of their possessions away from them. Yet none of this could stop a young white farmer named Abram Place.

Abram was just an ordinary young man who was looking for what most young men of the era wanted: a living and a suitable companion to share it with. Yet his heart was never captured by the American girls living in the town. Instead, he fell head over heels for a lovely young Ojibwe woman, whose name has been lost to history. Their love was forbidden; it would have been a society scandal of epic proportions, disapproved of by both his family and hers, but it couldn't stop either of them. Abram married her regardless, and he was wholly rejected by the majority of Peshtigo. He found himself living with a foot in both worlds, but at least he had a farm and a woman he loved to share it with.

The Ojibwe girl's relatives, however, eventually warmed to him. And this was likely what saved him from the devastation that was to come.

Abram Place was considered crazy by the rest of Peshtigo. Another person who may have found himself somewhat on the fringes of society was Father Peter Pernin.

A French-born Canadian Catholic missionary, Father Pernin may not have been entirely welcomed by the majority of the Peshtigo residents, who consisted mostly of Protestants. There were, however, still a few Catholics around. There were so few of them, though, that Father Pernin ministered not to one parish but to two: he traveled to and fro between Peshtigo and neighboring Marinette, which had a Catholic church. Peshtigo's Catholic church was still under construction.

Father Pernin himself was a sprightly man in his late forties who lived in a small home near the Peshtigo River. His house was sandwiched in the most unlikely of spaces, between the half-constructed church and the nearby saloon. He was planning to move to a newly-finished presbytery in Marinette shortly, as it was a larger town, but for now, he stayed in Peshtigo with his horse, dog, housekeeper, and pet blue jay.

Father Pernin felt that his mission was just starting to take off in Peshtigo and Marinette and that the future of Catholicism in both towns was bright.

Little did he know that their future, in general, was not bright. It was burning.

Chapter 3 – Ash Like Snow

Illustration II: A contemporary image from the Peshtigo Times

The fall of 1871 came to Peshtigo in all the usual glory of a fall in the northern woods. Among the dark splashes of the evergreen pines, deciduous trees turned ardent shades of bleeding red and blazing gold. The residents of Peshtigo were occupied with the busiest season of all: gathering blueberries, cutting hay, harvesting crops. But as

Thanksgiving approached, instead of gratitude, the people were filled with worry. The summer had not been kind to them.

A drought had come to Peshtigo with a strangling power that its residents had never seen before. Since July 8th of that year, there had been almost no rain whatsoever. September 5th saw only a pitiful little drizzle—a mere drop on the parched throat of the earth, nowhere near enough. The earth was wrung out, exhausted, spent.

For the people, drought was a dire and immediate crisis. Farmers like the Desrochers and Place families were faced with near disaster. Their cattle grew emaciated, their hips standing out like hat stands; even the best dairy cows had shrunken udders that yielded little milk. Crops were withering away and dying in the fields when they should have been bursting with plump cobs. The women and children gathered jars of pitiful little blackberries for the winter. The Ojibwe gathered cranberries from the flats that had been feeding their people for generations, but the harvest was sparse, and the people were faced with a winter of starvation.

For the Korstad family, Lars's work as a millwright had been largely complicated by the fact that there was great difficulty in getting the huge logs from the rugged northern reaches of the woods, where they had been cut, down to Peshtigo to be hewed by the lumberjacks. The millionaire owner of the sawmill and former first mayor of Chicago William Ogden had decided to float those logs down the Ohio River. But the drought had drained the water level to such an extent that the great rafts of logs couldn't make it through. Instead, they had to be brought down by beasts of burden, and it was a most inefficient method, leaving the Korstads preparing for an influx of logs that would come in the winter when iced tracks could be built and they could be brought down on sleds.

The forest itself looked like it was curling up and dying on the hills where it had marched since the Woodland Period. In the words of one anonymous resident, "The forests of pine were tinder, ready and anxious for suicide by fire. All nature was so dry and miserable that it cried out for death."

Father Pernin, too, felt there was something sinister about those woods. He had two close encounters with small fires that fall. Once, while out hunting for pheasant with a preteen boy as his guide, he and the boy found themselves lost—and soon surrounded by small flames. The boy's parents, luckily for them, came looking for them; they had to beat the flames down in order to give Father Pernin and the child a safe escape. Another time, while driving back and forth between his parishes, Father Pernin found himself confronted by a wall of flame on the side of the road. The smoke obscured the road so completely that he didn't know if he would be able to pass through safely. He decided that he had to try or risk being trapped by fire, and somehow, he managed to convince his horse to go through the smoke, where they emerged on the other side rattled but unscathed. Yet Father Pernin was worried that there would be more to come.

Still, life went on in the little town. It had to: there was nowhere else to go for most of its residents. They had already fled a life that they considered far worse than this, and there was no going back anymore. They continued with their preparations for winter as well as they could, hoping that they were going to survive it.

Part of that work included clearing land that could be farmed the next spring. Clearing land was an arduous task, and a never-ending one in the thick woods of the Wisconsin frontier. Crops and pastures couldn't be planted or seeded unless the wilderness had been beaten back. To the dismay of the watching Ojibwe, the pioneers had no reverence for the trees that had been growing there for untold centuries. They chopped them down even when they didn't need the lumber for their own homes or canoes. Piling up the brush, they sent the logs away to be processed at the mill, then burned the brush. It burned hot and quick, sparks flying in every direction until it had been consumed into patches of white ash on the blackened earth. Stumps were more difficult to deal with. There was no digging them out—those roots had been clinging to the earth for hundreds of years. Instead, the stumps were set alight, and they'd burn for days and days, smoldering away the lives of those ancient trees while sending little coals into the air.

Fires were inevitable. So, when small fires began to spring up throughout September of 1871, it was just another part of life on the frontier. Forest fires were nothing new, and with rudimentary methods, people usually managed to keep them away from their homes. Let them burn up the woods—it saved labor when clearing land. Growing forest fires began to pop up all the way from Canada to Iowa, but they burned themselves out eventually, at least according to the telegrams that were still coming into the town.

Things began to change by the end of September. The flat stillness of the drought began to give way to restless winds that shifted and pulled, driving fires ahead of them wherever they went. The air became frequently tainted with the smoke of distant fires, and still, the winds grew and grew. Elders in the town worried and began to stockpile water wherever they could, just in case. They hoped it would be enough. It wasn't.

The first great blow came at the very end of September. The fires that had been bursting out all over the woods reached out toward Green Bay, and the telegraph lines—a lifeline from Peshtigo, Green Bay, and Oconto to the rest of the universe—were destroyed. In one flash of fire, Peshtigo was utterly cut off from the cities surrounding it. Messages would have to travel on foot or by horseback now, and even those could seldom get through the wall of flames that was slowly but surely cutting Peshtigo off from the rest of the world. The fires were so devastating that great flocks of birds arrived in Peshtigo, fleeing from areas where their nests had been consumed by the flames.

* * * *

Sugar Bush was not so much a village as it was simply a scattered group of settlements, home to a couple of hundred families. It was barely a speck on the map in comparison to the 2,000-strong population of Peshtigo. The little knot of settlers was similar to the people of Peshtigo, as most of them were immigrants and farmers, many of them of German and French descent, who raised animals and crops and children on their land. They had lives, families, a little drama, and farms that they loved. Until October 7th, that is.

The fires that had been crackling and spreading throughout the forests were whipped wild by the wind, as uncontrollable and frenzied as lashed horses, and the isolated splashes of fire drove crazily across the forests until they finally found one another and grew into a single giant of towering flame. And it swept down upon Sugar Bush, mindless, merciless, and heedless of the little specks of humanity that raced around the trees it consumed so rapidly, fighting for their farms and then fleeing for their lives.

It was all to no avail. The families that lived and worked and loved there all died that night. Not one single Sugar Bush farm managed to escape the wrath of the blaze. They were all utterly consumed, annihilated in the fire, reduced to heaps of ash. The people who lived there tried to flee, but not even the best horse in Sugar Bush could outpace this disaster, and they were all reduced to nothing but bones, charred flesh, and ashes.

Where there had once been brightly painted barns now held only heaps of white ash. Trees were reduced to shriveled black skeletons sprawled in the dirt. Waving fields of crops were wiped clean away, leaving only scorched dirt. The jars full of blueberries that had been so carefully gathered were nothing but blobs of melted glass, and there were no hands left that could make them into pies anymore.

Sugar Bush was utterly gone, every one of its citizens killed by the wrathful speed of the blaze. And as the wind drove it ever on, an enormous low-pressure cell, which would have become a hurricane if there had been rainclouds to feed it, advanced on its next target: Peshtigo.

* * * *

October 8th, 1871, started like any other fall Sunday in Peshtigo for the majority of its residents. News about Sugar Bush hadn't reached them—how could it? Nobody was left alive in the settlement to tell them what had happened. The fires seemed to be dying down a little, and people began to hope that Peshtigo had been spared. So much of the woods had burned around them. Everyone knew that no fire could burn the same place twice. Perhaps Peshtigo would be spared.

The town was still wreathed in a gray shroud of smoke, but the winds seemed to have stilled a little, and so, the people went about another Sunday like they would do every Sunday.

Church was normally held in the evenings, giving families from far-flung areas time to get to the church, and this Sunday was no different. We could imagine, perhaps, that Lars and his wife were busy getting ready, excited for nine-day-old baby Anna to attend church for the very first time in the country that her parents had fought so hard to get to. The Villers, perhaps, were visiting family or relatives in Peshtigo with little Florence and their adopted son Joseph. Maybe Amelia Desrochers's mother was fretting over her five children and nursing her fevered husband in the little shack, contemplating the idea of skipping church that evening—how was she going to manage all those children and a sickly man? Their small worries were crowding them; how they would have discarded those worries if they had known what was coming!

For most people in Peshtigo, October 8th was a day of rest. Farmers did only the necessary tasks, feeding, watering, milking, mucking out, then putting up their feet for a few hours before church. Even the lumberjacks who worked up in the high camps among the trees came down into town for a day of drinking, womanizing, and perhaps picking a fight or two with the Ojibwe. It was a day to relax—except for Abram Place.

For Abram, it was everything but an ordinary Sunday, all thanks to his Ojibwe wife's relatives. The tribe had come to his peaceful farm on the outskirts of Peshtigo with wide eyes and terrible news. They told him that the fires were anything but finished, that in all their generations of living in this area and telling stories to their grandchildren—and hearing stories from their grandparents—they had never heard or seen anything like what they had witnessed in the destroyed settlement of Sugar Bush. This fire was not just an ordinary fire. It was a storm of flame, a rising, twirling thing driven wild by the wind, destroying all in its path, even ground that had already been burned.

They didn't tell the rest of the people in Peshtigo, or if they did, nobody believed them. They were just savages, after all, in the eyes of most people. Besides, the Ojibwe were not particularly inclined to lend a helping hand to the Americans. Those people had forced them out of the fertile land where they'd lived for decades; they were cutting down their ancient woods and trampling all over their sacred effigy mounds, tearing them up and planting crops where the bones of their ancestors once lay. Some Ojibwe even blamed the white people for the fires. This had never happened before, not until they came with their axes and plows and started tearing up the land.

But they told Abram Place because he was married to one of them and treated her well, and Abram took them seriously. Like the Ojibwe, he either didn't care to tell the rest of Peshtigo, or he did and nobody believed him when he said that the fire was coming and that it was coming on a scale that nobody had ever seen before. At any rate, when Abram hitched up whatever he used to plow his fields—mules or horses or oxen, perhaps—his neighbors thought he was a fool. It was the middle of fall, hardly time for plowing. Crazy Abram Place was just acting strange again. The man had married an Indian. What did he know?

Abram didn't let them stop him, though. Frantically, he began to tear up the area around his house, turning over the soil until there was nothing left for a fire to consume. The Ojibwe came to help him, perhaps by hand or perhaps with teams of their own, but either way, it was an endless and backbreaking task. What we achieve today in a few trips of a tractor was done in 1871 with a single plowshare, digging up a single line of dirt at a time. Abram must have worked non-stop all day to plow all the way around his house, and even then, the work wasn't done. The Ojibwe told him to get blankets and soak them in water, using them to cover his house and wet it down. Abram didn't question them. He began to do as they told.

Father Pernin spent a peaceful Sunday at home with his pets once he'd completed Mass in Marinette. The Peshtigo church was just about to be plastered, and it was in no condition to hold a mass that Sunday, so he went home instead and spent a pleasant afternoon on his porch, trying not to get too annoyed at the drunkards that lolled around in the saloon, picking fights with each other and uttering, in his words, "horrid blasphemies." Father Pernin listened to his blue jay singing instead and tried not to worry as smoke cloaked the town completely.

That evening, some of the people of Peshtigo headed to one of their churches, the Congregational Church. It had just been given its annual coat of white paint, and the red gleam of the distant fires reflected on it. The Korstads, the Villers, and maybe the Desrochers all headed to town on roads that had been paved with sawdust. At this time of year, it would have normally been keeping the roads from getting hopelessly muddy; now, it crunched under their feet, dry as tinder in the drought. Stepping off the sawdust road (perhaps Amelia's short legs struggled a little with this part), they would climb up onto wooden sidewalks and pass by buildings that had all been built with timber frames, logs, or planks for the walls and wooden shingles for the roof. Peshtigo was a tinderbox waiting for a spark.

It is highly unlikely that Abram Place went to church that Sunday. Perhaps he never went to church at all; he was probably unwelcomed there, thanks to his Ojibwe wife. Either way, he was too busy draping wet blankets over his house to head into town.

The sermon was delivered as usual. The pastor had been rather fond of themes of infernal fire for the past few weeks, perhaps hoping that the threat of earthly fire would make his parishioners think twice about their lifestyles, especially the lumberjacks. When it was over, they all stepped out of the church onto their wooden sidewalks and sawdust streets, and the smoke was so thick that they could barely see across the street. It was hot and choking, burning their throats and lungs, perhaps making baby Anna cry. And through the smoke, something fell in small white flakes, piling onto the ground and onto the men's hats and the women's bonnets.

It wasn't snow. It was ash.

Chapter 4 – Nature Lifted up Its Voice

The tumbling ash fell slowly, unhurried by the wind; in fact, a stillness had come over the entire town, with not a breath of air stirring the clouds of smoke that hung over everything. Families hurried back to their homes, telling each other that it was a good thing the wind had died down. All Peshtigo had dodged a bullet, they said. If only they knew that bullet was still on its way and heading straight for them.

With ash settling on their shoulders and in the hair of the little girls, the families went home. Evening came, but darkness did not fall. The whole city was lit up in a red haze from the distant fires; the stars were hidden by the smoke, and the stench of it was everywhere. Even the streetlamps glowed sickly green-yellow in the smoke.

And then the wind rose.

The smoke curled and swirled before it as it rushed through the town, huffing its hot breath down the backs of necks and into faces, rustling the curtains, sending an ominous howl through the eaves of the stores and among the whipping branches of the trees as leaves and pine needles and sand scattered before it. The ash that coated everything was blown into the finest white powder and driven everywhere. The unease that had settled in the hearts of the townsfolk, thick as smoke, was driven into something that verged upon panic. To make matters worse, the smoke was not constant. It blew in unhappy puffs, roaring one moment and resting the next. One would just begin to believe that the wind had died down completely when it came thrusting at one again from an unexpected angle, pulling at hats and clothes, coughing smoke.

Some men decided it was time to take further action. Volunteers hurried to the street corners, carrying barrels and tin bathtubs of water, setting them down strategically. Others came out with shovels and pails—it was all that they had with which to face the blaze that was coming.

Father Pernin, too, felt uncomfortable with the wind that gusted against the windows of his little home. His housemaid, who must have lived with him, was restless as she prepared his dinner. The blue jay was no longer singing. Father Pernin began to worry about his neighbor—not the ungainly bunch of men who were still carousing merrily in the saloon but an elderly widow on the other side, Mrs. Dress. Her children had a habit of writing off her concerns and ignoring her, and the priest decided she needed a friend in a time like this. He walked over to her home and asked if she was all right. Mrs. Dress was not all right. She was worried, and as Father Pernin had suspected, her children laughed at her when she begged them to do something.

The priest invited Mrs. Dress to take a walk with him—perhaps they could see more from an open field on her land. They headed off together, the staunch priest perhaps offering his strong arm to the elderly widow, and made their way to where they could see part of the woods. At first, the danger seemed to be only moderate, which was normal for the fire season. The smoke obscured everything; there was a red glow across the sky, but it seemed distant enough.

But the wind rose again. This time it blew with a hot vehemence that took Father Pernin's breath away. Mrs. Dress clung to his arm as the wind roared across the clearing, rustling the dry branches of a series of old, dead tree trunks. As the horrified priest watched, the trunks—without a sign of a spark—suddenly burst into flame. They must have been smoldering deep inside, and the wind was just the fan they needed. The next thing Father Pernin knew, the flames were roaring around them, sparks flying onto the dry grass of the fields. Mrs. Dress was crying out in fear. Father Pernin ran for water and flung pails of it onto the roaring flames; somehow, he managed to extinguish the trees.

Coughing, his eyes streaming from the smoke, Father Pernin turned to Mrs. Dress and told her that the fire was coming for them. They had to take all the precautions they could.

As Father Pernin hurried back into the town, he could hear the church bells ringing all around them. There was a distant sound, only occasionally audible when the gusts of wind died down. It was a kind of roar; it sounded as if the forest itself had grown a red maw and was bellowing its rage upon the men who encroached upon it. Later, he would write, "The silence of the tomb reigned among the living; nature alone lifted up its voice and spoke."

Father Pernin ran into his house. He was acutely aware of one thing: the tabernacle of the Peshtigo church. Since the church wasn't done yet, the tabernacle was in his home for safekeeping, and it contained the holiest of all holy things in a Catholic priest's eyes: the Blessed Sacrament, the Eucharist. He couldn't let anything happen to it. He had to protect it as well as he could.

The priest's garden was of soft, sandy soil, and his arms were strong. He decided that the best course of action would be to dig a trench across it to form a kind of firebreak if he could; the river was also close by, but it would have to be Plan B. Hurrying outside, Father Pernin was distracted by the hollow noise of hooves on wood. His horse, trapped in his stable, was hurrying this way and that, kicking at the walls, his breaths coming in short snorts of terror. Father Pernin hesitated for a moment. If the trench didn't work, he could hitch his wagon to the horse or even scramble onto his back and ride for safety much faster than his own two legs could carry him. That horse could save his life. But if the worst happened, if the fire was too quick for Father Pernin, then the animal would be consumed by flames and perish in his stable. Father Pernin couldn't let that happen. He ran to the stable, drew back the bolts, and threw the door wide open. The horse lunged onto the street and galloped away from the flames, tail thrown high, hooves hammering on the road as he disappeared into the woods. Father Pernin could only pray that the animal hadn't taken his last hope of survival with him.

Father Pernin's housemaid was running around madly as he headed to the garden, carrying baskets of silverware from the house, hardly knowing where she'd take them. He called out to her and told her to flee. She ran back into the house, reemerging with her most precious possession, a cage containing her pet canary. The little bird was chirping and fluttering in terror. When she stepped outside, a roar of wind rushed through the town, seizing the cage and flinging it high into the air. The maid screamed for Father Pernin to flee and then ran away herself, leaving him alone in his garden, digging frantically in a bid to save the tabernacle.

Father Pernin wasn't the only one racing to protect everything he loved. Adam Place felt the wind on his skin grow chill where his clothes had been soaked by the water he was using to try to keep his home too wet for the flames to take. Ojibwe tribesmen swarmed over the house, floundering in the deeply plowed fields, rushing from the well to the home and back with blankets in their hands. A trail of damp earth led from the well to the house. Soot and ash, mixing with the water, smeared over everyone's skin until it was impossible to see the difference between the white American and the Native Americans. And there was no difference, not now, not in the face of the great snapping roar that had grown distantly audible beyond the treetops.

Adam paused on the roof of his house, another wet blanket lying at his feet where he'd laid it down, acutely aware of his young and lovely wife as she rushed around like the rest of them. He looked over his shoulder, back into the woods, and the plumes of smoke were moving faster. The sound was unlike anything he'd experienced before. The wind was howling, yes, but this was different. This wasn't the sound of the wind. This was a deep, full-throated bellow, the tortured roar of a distraught landscape faced with its doom. Something was glowing in the distance, cloaked by the smoke. It was bright scarlet, throbbing. It seemed to be spinning. And it was coming right at them.

Abram turned back to his work with renewed terror. The Ojibwe had been right: this was no ordinary fire. He had never seen anything like this before.

* * * *

Back in Peshtigo, Father Pernin heard the roar too. It had been an undertone to the afternoon's struggle; now, it was rising up above all of the other sounds, and panic had gripped the town in its cold fingers. Sweat poured down the priest's face, his muscles aching, lungs burning with smoke, as he struggled to finish the trench. When he moved back toward the house, the sight that greeted him was almost surreal, as if his work had driven him directly into a nightmare.

The quiet street was packed. Sawdust and soot blew in all directions as droves of people and animals fled, yet there were no screams. The people seemed to have been robbed of their ability to protest their fate; instead, they were reduced to a frightened pack of prey animals, silent in their quest for safety. Families were clinging together, children holding their mother's skirts, parents clutching babies close. Men struggled to handle frightened horses that would have turned their carts over in their flight. And the house cats. Father Pernin was familiar with the sight of them dodging around town, lapping up saucers of milk in kitchens, flitting in and out of view in the barns. But now they moved down the street like an army, like a wolf pack, a crowd of cats rushing out of reach of the approaching blaze.

Some of the braver men were running in the other direction to join the handful of courageous volunteers who'd hurried to the edge of town to face the fire, but Father Pernin could see that it was utterly useless. The trench he'd been digging for hours looked like a foolish and futile thing now as well. He knew he had to flee. He ran for the house, his heart pounding, desperate to save the one thing that was most precious to him, the holy tabernacle containing the Blessed Sacrament.

Miles away, in a tiny shack on their farm, the Desrochers family had long since gone to bed. Charles, the father, had been sleeping most of the day thanks to his illness, Mrs. Desrochers was worn out by the endless demands of her growing family, and little Amelia was curled up on her simple bed. She was fast asleep when something—perhaps the devastating sound, perhaps the choking smoke that had filled the shack and burned her lungs—woke her mother. Mrs. Desrochers rushed to the window and stared at a world that had been suddenly and horribly enveloped in flame. The woods all around them were burning, the deafening crackle of the blaze heralding the arrival of sheets of flame that reduced entire branches to nothing in the few moments that Mrs. Desrochers was looking. Half-asleep, she could hardly comprehend what she was seeing.

"Charles!" she cried. "Wake up! The end of the world is coming! Everything's on fire!"

Charles was sleepy and didn't feel well. He turned over, ignoring the woman's cries. "Go to bed. Go to bed," he groaned. "You're dreaming."

Amelia was awake now, sitting up, frightened by the terror in her mother's voice. She watched as her mother ran to her father's bed, shaking him, pleading him to come to the window and see for himself. Annoyed, Charles lurched to his feet and lumbered to the window, where he was stricken by the sight of their entire farm ablaze. "Oh, Mother!" he gasped to his wife. "You're right. Everything *is* on fire. I must be dreaming too."

Mrs. Desrochers had woken up thoroughly by this time, and she was aware that there was no time for speculation. The devouring flames would swallow their shack in a gulp. She rushed to her children and started pulling them out of bed, calling to the older ones that it was time to get dressed. Amelia was tugged to her feet. The next thing she knew, her hard, little cheap shoes were being thrust onto her feet, the laces tied without any stockings. There wasn't time for stockings, and besides, the blaze had turned the chilly fall night into a baking inferno.

Amelia's father was shouting over the roar now, telling them that they had to get down to the river as fast as their legs could carry them; he would try to save the house if he could. Her mother didn't question him. She grabbed her children and fled.

In the millwright's shanty, the smoke and the sound of the fire had woken baby Anna. Her tiny lungs generated high-pitched screams of terror. When Lars Korstad sat up on his sawdust bed, he knew at once that the shanty had become a death trap.

Lars got his wife to her feet, crying for her to take the baby as he grabbed a bucket. They had to make for the river, he told his wife. It would be their only hope of surviving. His wife's eyes were wide with terror as she hugged her wailing baby close to her. She couldn't bear to think of little Anna's life being cut so cruelly short by something so violent.

In the house where the Villers were staying, another baby was crying—their treasured little Florence. Joseph found himself being shaken awake. The frightened voices of his adoptive parents told him that they had to flee to somewhere safe. Octavia was swaddling Florence in whatever blankets were closest to hand, stuffing the little one into a wicker basket and tucking her in as safely as she could. Calling to the teenager, Martin and Octavia ran out of the house.

Joseph was hot on their heels. As soon as he stepped outside, the roaring wind snatched at him, throwing hot ash and heat against him: the gales were pumping at over a hundred miles an hour that night. The cool, starlit woods he so dearly loved had been transformed into a raging whirl of confusion, heat, and terror. The sound was deafening, and when Joseph looked up, he saw that the woods were already engulfed in flames. Sheets of fire two hundred feet high towered over the little family, the licking flames devouring the woods as they leaped from tree to tree, coming ever closer to the house. Already the flames were only yards from the home. Florence was crying her little lungs out.

Octavia placed the basket down at the edge of the garden. Shouting to Joseph to stay where he was, she and Martin turned around and ran back into the house to get something —Joseph didn't know what. Before he could call for them to come back, they'd both disappeared into the house. It was only for a moment, but a moment was enough.

The howling wind seized a smoldering piece of bark and hurled it across the grassy meadow in front of the house. Joseph started forward, but that little speck of flame had already touched the ground. In a bare instant, a line of fire roared up between them, separating him utterly from the house and his adoptive parents.

There was fire all around him, and smoke churned above him. No matter how hard he screamed their names, Martin and Octavia did not answer. There was just the yelling of the baby, and Joseph ran to her, scooping her into his arms, clinging to her tiny body as the blaze surrounded him.

They were alone.

Chapter 5 – A Holocaust of Fire

Illustration III: An artist's depiction of victims of the fire seeking refuge in the river

Feverishly working at protecting his home, Abram Place was not yet ready to accept that the end of the world had come. As his home swarmed with Ojibwe, their helping hands thrusting water onto everything that was valuable, he continued to work side by side with them to save his home and lands. Being one of the wealthiest landowners in the town—albeit its most judged pariah—wasn't going to help him now. Only his friends, the Ojibwe, and his stubborn determination would keep him going.

And he clung on to the hope that his home would be saved, but deep into the night, Abram witnessed something that made him quake in his very boots.

The roar was coming closer and closer. It had reached an almost unthinkable volume, and that was when the firestorm came into sight. Wrapped in wisps of pitch-black smoke, a great twisting tower of fire stormed down upon the Place home, moving with a speed that Abram could barely comprehend. Its proportions were those of the biblical pillar of flame, but instead of guiding, this fire did nothing except destroy. It threw great tongues of flame all over the woods, sending them chasing each other madly among the trees like hunting dogs, as the firestorm itself marched past, a whirling devil of utter destruction. Some would later describe it as a "firenado"; it certainly looked just like a tornado, except this tornado burned.

Somehow, the firestorm passed by Abram's home, likely helped by the extensive measures he'd taken to protect it. But Peshtigo itself was not so lucky. Its residents would soon find themselves trapped in the belly of the firestorm.

* * * *

Father Pernin's blue jay wasn't silent anymore. The little bird chirped in panic, beating its wings on the bars of its cage, as its owner ran through the house. Everything was so obscured with smoke that Father Pernin could barely find his way to where the tabernacle stood in his room. Pulling a key out of his coat, Father Pernin tried to unlock the wooden box, but in his haste, it clattered from his hands. The flames were roaring close by now; his house was all but on fire. There was no time to look for it. He grabbed the box in his arms and ran back downstairs to where his buggy was waiting, fighting against the howling wind that threatened to yank him off his feet as it hurled soot and smoke in his face. The horse had long gone, but he couldn't carry the heavy tabernacle all the way on his own. Even then, he wouldn't abandon the Blessed Sacrament. He flung it onto the buggy and jumped between the shafts himself.

Father Pernin's earlier exhaustion after digging the trench had been replaced with an adrenalin-fueled strength that he didn't know he had. Straightening, he lifted the buggy into position and began to move, dragging it behind him as if he himself were a horse. The buggy was light, and he was strong, and they made good progress. As he headed for the fence that surrounded his home, a great gust of wind blew from the center of the fire, and it was so powerful that it yanked the whole fence and the gate from the ground and flung them down across the street.

Many men would have abandoned the buggy there and then and run for safety. But for Father Pernin, a strange calm seemed to settle over him. He would later describe his state of mind as "childlike" in its lack of panic. As he watched his fence being torn up and scattered before the blaze like a heap of twigs, all he could think was that at least now he wouldn't have to stop and open the gate. All he had to do was run. And run he did, the buggy rattling and bouncing beside him, his feet crunching in the sawdust as he made for the river.

He was not the only one who was rushing to seek solace in the cold waters of the Peshtigo. In fact, the streets were still crowded with fleeing people, but their desperation now was ten times that of the crowd that had gone before when Father Pernin was still busy digging his trench. Families struggled along, parents clutching their children, couples clinging to each other, and loose animals stampeded among them, frightened horses trampling on unheeding children, cattle knocking people out of their way as they rushed toward safety.

The conditions were utterly appalling. The smoke was so thick that it was almost impossible to breathe and often impossible to see; Father Pernin half-felt his way through the gray cloud, thick as the fear that hung in the air around him. He could barely hear the labored rasp of his own breathing or the thump of his feet on the ground. Strong as he was, and fit as he was, he was able to keep going, buggy and all. Others were struggling more; they ran a few steps, then lay down to breathe the cooler air near the road before running on again as fast as those breaths would fuel them.

At last, Father Pernin heard the rush of water and realized he'd finally reached the river. Rushing up to the edge, he looked out hopefully at what should have been a smooth slope down to the slow-moving waters. Instead, he was faced with an appalling sight. The sawmill on the other bank of the river was afire. Whipping tongues of flame licked around it, leaping across to the buildings left and right. The fire did not seem to be tied to any source of fuel; it surged before the wind as if it found something to burn in the air itself. These tongues of flame roared and rustled so high, pushed so hard by the wind, that they crossed the very river itself. Reflected brilliantly in the water, they had nearly reached the bank where Father Pernin was standing. Logs had tumbled loose from their stores upriver; they floated down on the water now, burning, their flames illuminating panicked animals that swam though the current alongside them. The people who had been desperate enough to fling themselves into the river regardless were being knocked this way and that by the animals and the logs; that was if the flames leaping over the river didn't get them first. Worse, when Father Pernin raised his eyes to the wooden bridge leading into Peshtigo, he saw that it was burning. It would be only moments before it collapsed into the river.

Even now, somehow, the priest failed to lose his cool. Going downriver was impossible thanks to the bridge and the flames. He would just have to head farther up the river instead. Turning, he followed the bank, laboring under the weight of the buggy yet somehow managing to keep going with the heavy tabernacle on board behind him.

Eventually reaching a place where the banks were not too steep to go in, Father Pernin made for the water. The ice-cold water sloshed around his ankles as he pulled and pulled at the buggy, struggling to get the wheels to move in the mud. At last, he managed to get the buggy into the water. When he looked up, the trees above the river were all aflame. The sight sent a burst of strength through him. With all his heart, he believed that he had to get the tabernacle to safety, come what may. The wind swirled the water around his hips and chest, pulling at his hair, trying to knock him off his feet as he kept pulling on the buggy until, at last, he could pull no more. The tabernacle, he hoped, would be safe where it was.

Clinging to the sturdy shape of his buggy as it rocked in the endless gusts of wind, Father Pernin prepared to hunker down and stay where he was. Every muscle in his body burned; he could hardly breathe, struggling to suck down gulps of air that were tainted with the thick and toxic smoke. The roar of the wind had brought a fresh explosion of flame to the opposite bank. The spot where he'd stood just moments ago had already been engulfed in rippling flames, and all over, all around, all above him, the world was on fire. The heat was blistering against his face.

Looking up, Father Pernin saw that he was not alone. Others had rushed to the bank at this spot, and they were just feet away from the cool sanctuary of water, but in the unnatural bright light of the fire, which was brighter than day, he saw that many of them were rooted to the spot. Mouths open, tongues protruding, eyes popping, they stared up at the wall of fire that was rushing upon them and failed to flee. He could only think that they believed the world had ended and that there was no use in fighting their inevitable fate.

But Father Pernin, man of God though he was, was also a man of logic. If the world was ending, he reasoned, God would probably have told him before this point. There was hope yet. He scrambled up the riverbank once more and rushed at the nearest man who was standing on the bank and staring at the oncoming wall of death. When Father Pernin tried to speak, he found it was impossible; the priest had barely enough breath left to keep himself moving. Instead, he just grabbed the man's clothes—they already burned to the touch—and flung him into the river with a mighty splash. Braving the flames,

Father Pernin kept going, pushing men, women, and children alike into the water. The cold water seemed to have a reviving effect on them; they spluttered, clung to each other, and made their way deeper into the river to avoid the flames as they came back to life. All but one man. When Father Pernin shoved this man into the shallow water, the man struggled back out feebly, his mind addled by smoke inhalation. "I'm wet," he said.

Father Pernin had neither the time nor the breath to argue with him. He shoved him again, and this time, the man stayed put.

When he could no longer move along the riverbank, Father Pernin scrambled back into the river again, and the frightened fellow victims of the blaze began to wade over to him and cluster around him. Perhaps they recognized their savior or just believed they might be safer somehow near a priest. Squinting against the smoke, Father Pernin could no longer see the buggy and tabernacle.

Now that he was able to breathe a little more, Father Pernin realized how hot his face was. In fact, with tongues of fire curling through the air above him, it felt as though the air itself was ablaze. A spark struck his shoulder, a tiny flame curling on the cloth of his coat. Father Pernin submerged himself, feeling the blessed cool of the water on his face. When he resurfaced, spluttering, he pulled off his coat and put it over his head. Around him, others failed to have that presence of mind; instead, they stared at him, bewildered, as their clothes began to smoke on them.

A scrap of something floated past, and Father Pernin grabbed it. It was a quilt, charred at the edges, but still useful; he tried not to think of what could have happened to its owner. Pulling it out of the water, he flung it over the head of the nearest person. More and more things were floating toward him—hats and bits of blanket and coats—and he pulled them from the water and started covering the people's heads around him.

One of them grabbed at him, her eyes desperate. She asked him if it was the end of the world.

It certainly felt that way. Looking up, Father Pernin could no longer see the sky; the whole world seemed to have become a billowing ball of flame. Even the water surrounding them, reflecting the fire, was glowing.

"I don't think so," he told her, "but if other countries are burned as ours seems to have been, the end of the world, at least for us, must be at hand."

They didn't talk after that. They just huddled together in the frigid water and watched the world burn.

* * * *

All over Peshtigo, people were abandoning their homes, farms, and sometimes even families in their desperate quest for safety. For many of them, this attempt would be futile. Fleeing through the smoke and flames, families were faced with difficult terrain as they floundered through the woods in search of refuge. The firestorm grew in strength and speed; it would cover miles in minutes, sometimes outpacing the fleeing families. The heat roared up to several thousand degrees, and trees—and sometimes human bodies—exploded at the touch of the fire. Whole families were consumed in a single lick of flame. Many people were struck down and burned alive in their tracks, reduced to ashes before they could even know what had happened to them. Children, their parents robbed of them by tongues of flame, ran panicking through the woods, screaming their names.

Among those fleeing the fire were the little Korstad family. Strong Lars, his hand gripping his wife's, half dragged her after him as she carried baby Anna. He still clutched the bucket in his hand, praying that they would get to a water source so that he could use it. The air was so hot that it blistered his cheeks and the back of his neck as he fled down toward the river. It was at their very heels, the little flames licking around the dry undergrowth at their feet, but Lars did not give up. Begging, pleading his wife to keep going, ignoring the distressed screams of the baby, he kept running.

At last, they saw the glimmer of light reflected on the water, and they burst out of the woods to find the river winding through its bed before them. Lars and his wife crashed into the soothing water. Already the banks were ablaze; they had to go in deeper, and Lars despaired. His wife was still weak after the birth, and the baby was so small.

It's unclear where Lars found the raft. Perhaps he had time to make it, although it seems unlikely. It is more probable that another family had been forced to abandon it. Either way, Lars somehow got his hands onto a raft that had been covered with a feather mattress. Considering that the mattresses in his own home were stuffed with sawdust, it's unlikely that this was something he'd brought with him from the shanty. Regardless of where it came from, the raft was a lifesaver. Lars scrambled onto it, pulling his wife and baby up alongside him, floating it out into the center of the river.

Even there, as Father Pernin had discovered, they weren't safe. The trees were spitting sparks and blazing cinders across the water; if they landed on the raft, the whole thing would go up in flames, taking the Korstad family with it. Lars tucked the baby safely into his wife's arms and told her to hold baby Anna tightly. Then he plunged the bucket deep into the river, drawing up lifegiving scoops of water. Pouring it over his wife and child, Lars kept working, bringing up bucketful after bucketful in a desperate bid to keep them alive. The clothes on his back were burning, and his wife's skirt kept catching fire between bucketfuls. The flames were so hot that they dried their clothes almost instantly, steam rising from them. But there was nothing else Lars could do. So, he just kept on trying to keep his wife and baby alive.

* * * *

Far from the comparative safety of the river, Joseph LaCrosse stared in voiceless horror at the wall of flame that now separated him from the house in which Martin and Octavia had disappeared. Little Florence was screaming, her tiny fists clutching at his shirt as he stared at the flames, and there was a roaring noise rushing upon them that made Joseph aware that even worse was to come. His cries for help had been fruitless; he was utterly isolated by the roaring flames. The boy was only fourteen. What could he do alone?

But being alone was nothing new to Joseph. His parents had long since been lost, and he was used to making his own decisions. The most important thing he had to do was to take care of little Florence. Clinging to her as tightly as he could, Joseph looked this way and that, searching for any form of shelter. His eyes rested on a well. In those days, piped water was reserved for cities—most farmers had to have their own wells, from which they drew up water in a bucket. The farm where the Villers were staying was no different. The well was just a few yards away from Joseph and Florence.

Joseph made his choice quickly. Holding the baby with all his strength, he ran for the well. The stone wall surrounding it must have already been searing to the touch; climbing down that black pit, a deadly drop to the water below him, while holding an upset baby, must have been a nearly impossible task. Somehow, though, Joseph managed it. He slipped down into the water, holding Florence close, and feeling that it had already turned warmer than usual. When he looked up, the firestorm was upon them. The mouth of the well was completely engulfed in burning flames, illuminating the rippling water, the boy's blistered hands, and the tearful, screaming face of little Florence. There was nowhere else to go. Joseph curled himself around the baby, keeping them both in the water, and could only hope that he'd be safe where he was.

Many people had thought similarly to Joseph and climbed down into wells or water tanks, and many of them perished horribly. The heat of the fire was such that even great cisterns of water could be brought to a boil, cooking its inhabitants alive. Others were simply dried up completely, and the fire consumed all that hid within. Joseph could feel the danger coming upon him, but there was nothing he could do but hold onto Florence and wait.

* * * *

Mrs. Desrochers's hand was slippery with sweat, but somehow, she kept her grip on little Amelia's arm as she raced through the woods.

The little girl's feet slid around uncomfortably in her shoes; she cried out for rest, but the smoke surrounding them choked her words, and her mother was not about to slow down—not with a spinning tower of fire roaring down upon them, a harbinger of certain death. It would appear that Charles had abandoned the useless bid to save their home. Now, all of the Desrochers were running for the river, crashing through the woods, scrambling over fallen logs. Branches and undergrowth snatched at them, all but invisible in the smoky air.

Amelia's little legs could take no more of the running when, at last, the river lay before them. A great barge, its hulking shape a welcome blessing in the dark, was making its way through the water. The captain shouted to them to come onto the boat: it was heading out onto Green Bay itself, where surely it would be safe.

It sounded like a good plan. The Desrochers rushed up to the riverbank, scrambling their way onto the barge, the parents and their five children making it onto the boat. Panting, clinging to Amelia, Mrs. Desrochers must have thought that they were out of danger now as the barge headed downriver as fast as it could possibly go.

She was horribly mistaken. The fire was at the very banks now, snapping at their heels, and the burning trees were casting bits of cinders and fiery pieces of bark into the air. Fire rained down onto the barge, and it caught on fire. Screaming in panic, many occupants of the barge launched themselves overboard and into the river, but it was deep and fast-flowing, and they were unprepared for the cold. Amelia saw many of them go under, never to surface again. The Desrochers stayed, clinging to hope, as the men frantically struggled to put out the flames on their burning boat.

At last, the flames were quenched, and somehow, the barge found itself leaving behind the burning river for the blessed expanse of water that was Green Bay. Cool air surrounded them, soothing Amelia's burned and blistered face as the barge headed out onto the water, which had been whipped wild by the wind. Spray dashed against her, wonderfully cold and refreshing.

They were three miles out onto the bay when Amelia turned around to look back at the place that had once been their home. The firestorm had rushed through the whole of Peshtigo, reducing the entire town to nothing but ash, in less than a single hour. Now, it towered above the bay, awful in every sense of the word, plumes of smoke pouring into the air as the pillar of flame burned itself out against the water. Fire reigned all around them, but on the barge, at least, they were safe at last.

Little Amelia had almost no concept of what was really happening. She was largely unhurt, and her mother was with her, cradling her in her arms as they both stared up at what had become of their beloved woods. Cinders and ash were pouring out of the sky; they fluttered down on Amelia's outstretched hands, settling thickly on her eyelashes, in her tangled hair.

"Mother," she said, amazed. "Look! It's snowing fire."

Mrs. Desrochers said nothing. She just held her daughter and watched the world burn.

Chapter 6 – Among the Ashes

Father Pernin spent nearly six hours submerged in the ravaged waters of the Peshtigo, but it must have felt like an eternity. It felt as though the very air would boil; heat and smoke assailed all of his senses as he kept trying to keep those around him as wet as he could. He kept splashing water over his head and the heads of the people surrounding him, many of whom were too panicked or too weak to do so themselves. The heat simply evaporated the water almost instantaneously. They had to keep on splashing and splashing, as the hours wore on and the blaze still bellowed.

The firestorm itself passed through the whole of Peshtigo, razing most of it to the ground, in less than an hour. But its offspring, the small fires that slowly devoured whatever was left of the frontier town, kept on burning with such heat that the only safe place to be was within the waters of the river. As the hours ticked by, the conditions began to take their toll even on strong young Father Pernin. He had already been breathless when he first took to the river, and matters only grew worse with every burning lungful of smoky air. His attempts to help others and himself became more and more feeble.

At last, though, the priest realized that his face no longer felt like it was on fire. He slowed down, splashing less and less. The air was definitely cooler; in fact, everything felt cooler. Looking up, Father Pernin saw that the sky was no longer covered in fire. The worst of the blaze had passed them. Absolutely exhausted, his legs numb with the cold, Father Pernin groped for a nearby log. It was charred and blackened but not actively burning, and when he touched it, he found that he could pull himself up onto it. Draped over the log, his legs dangling in the water, Father Pernin hoped he could rest at last.

But the priest and those who had already survived the first roar of the blaze was about to discover that the most dangerous part of that night was still to come. The horrific truth of that tragic day was that almost as many people perished of cold as burned to death. The chill fall wind, lacking the hot breath of the flames now, struck straight through Father Pernin's soaked clothes, dragging its frigid fingers across his skin. He began to shiver uncontrollably, barely able to keep hold of the log, his throat and chest feeling more and more closed with every passing minute. His thoughts grew sluggish and feeble due to the lack of oxygen and freezing cold.

A young man—it was still too dark and smoky and awful for him to know who—saw the priest's plight and did what he could for him, draping a blanket over Father Pernin's shoulders. The warmth was just enough to stir him to full wakefulness. When he sat up a little, still clinging to the rough surface of the log, Father Pernin realized that the riverbank was no longer on fire. There was nothing left for it to burn; the sawmill that had been so splendid on the bank there had been reduced to nothing but rubble and ash, with only the iron hoops of barrels still whole. Struggling to wade on his numb legs, the priest made his way to the riverbank.

There were still some small fires burning here and there, and Father Pernin stumbled over to one of them, hoping to get some warmth from it. Cruelly, the flames could only dry the outer layers of his clothes, failing to warm his sodden underclothes and his trembling body. The priest couldn't call for help. His throat was swollen tight with smoke inhalation, and he could hardly breathe, let alone speak. In fact, he couldn't do anything at all. His strength failed him, and he collapsed face-down on the riverbank, semi-conscious and unable to move.

Hundreds of people perished in Peshtigo in the small hours of the morning on October 9th, their skin untouched but their lungs charred by the burning air they'd been forced to breathe. Others never made it out of the river; hypothermia took them swiftly and silently, a far more creeping and insidious killer than the firestorm itself. Father Pernin was suffering from both where he lay, and he could have easily died there. But he was one of the lucky ones. He had collapsed on the sand beside a small fire, and the heat of the firestorm had seeped deep into the riverbank. The sand was warm—warm enough that, after lying there for an indeterminable amount of time, Father Pernin began to recover. He found that he could move, and he pulled off his sodden shoes and socks, pressing the soles of his bare feet against the warm sand. It revived him somewhat, and that was when he realized how much pain he was in.

Though he hadn't been touched by the flames, the priest's face had been burned by the hot air; he hadn't known it earlier, as he was distracted by the tightness in his chest and the cold, but now, his eyes were shooting swift pangs of agony through his very skull. When he tried to open them, he found that they were swollen almost shut. With misty, filmy vision, Father Pernin tried to look around for help, but he seemed to be surrounded by nothing but death and destruction. Bodies lay all around him, charred beyond recognition. Some were draped over the iron hoops he'd noticed earlier among the sawmill. When he reached for one of the hoops, he found that it burned to the touch. At first, the stricken priest thought that the bodies lying on the hoops were men who'd tried to warm themselves against the iron. He would later find out that they'd already been dead when well-meaning fellow citizens had tried to lift them out of reach of the river and discovered that the bodies were so badly burned that they almost fell apart when touched by human hands. The hoops had proved to be the easiest way to move them.

Horrified, Father Pernin stared at a world that he barely recognized, even though he'd walked along this riverbank a thousand times. The world was shrouded in smoke. A grayness in the distance suggested that dawn was breaking, but everything was hidden behind the haze.

An instinct for survival saved him from the dismay somehow. Father Pernin realized that he was still freezing, still wet to the skin. There was no time now for dignity. He tossed aside the decorum that became a Catholic priest and began to pull off his clothes one by one, stripping to his very skin and standing naked by one of the fires. The warmth was delicious as he held out his clothes to dry, but it was little consolation. With every flicker of the flames, Father Pernin could see less and less. He'd survived both fire and water. But he was going slowly, horribly, and painfully blind.

* * * *

When the world had turned from swirls of flame to a desolate wasteland of black stumps and gray smoke, Lars Korstad could finally bring his stricken little family to the shore. He stumbled off the raft, his feet crunching on the blackened remnants of what had once been undergrowth, and held out his arms to his wife. She was faint, almost unconscious with strain, exhaustion, and smoke inhalation, but she was still alive. Yet he was afraid. The baby had gone very quiet.

Looking at his wife, Lars sadly noted that his attempts to save her and the baby by pouring river water over them had been woefully inadequate. The young woman's clothes had been burned from her very back. Her hair was screwed up, blackened by the heat; her dress had peeled away from her, leaving her half-naked in the slowly growing light of a darkened dawn. Where the flames had wrenched her clothes away from her, his wife's skin was red and blistered. She still clutched the little bundle in her arms.

Lars himself was throbbing all over from burns to his face and back, but he was more worried about the youngest member of their small family. He touched his wife. Trembling, she opened her arms, and his heart turned over.

His wife had used her body as a shield, and it had worked. The baby, curled up snugly in her blankets, slept soundly at her mother's breast, whole and unharmed.

* * * *

Joseph had to wait for a long time in that well as he held Florence, staying there even after the sky was no longer filled with flames above him. When he tried to start climbing up, he found that the sides of the well were so hot that he could hardly touch them. Florence couldn't understand. She screamed and cried as Joseph tried his best to keep her from falling into the water or touching the hot sides herself.

At last, though, when gray daylight began to penetrate the well, Joseph reached up and touched the wall of the well to find that it was just cool enough to grab on to. His strength was all but spent from the hours and hours he'd been holding that baby. It's unclear how deep the well was, or how Joseph kept his head above the water; whether he had something to cling on to or was standing in the water all that time, he must have been absolutely exhausted. Yet somehow, he managed to clamber out, keeping Florence tightly in one arm, and found himself in a world that he didn't recognize.

Everything was gone. The great woods that had surrounded him in a wall of majestic fall color had disappeared, replaced by a blackened wasteland, leveled almost to the ground except for a few sooty stumps that still smoldered in the gray morning. The house had been razed to the ground. It was as if it had never been there before. All the landmarks that Joseph knew, the beauty he'd seen around him just the day before, had disappeared. He may as well have stepped out onto some alien and inhospitable planet.

There was nothing else that seemed to be alive wherever Joseph looked except for the baby, who kept wailing. Just ashes and the little bones of small woodland animals. Joseph couldn't see bigger bones anywhere, and neither could he see Martin and Octavia. They were gone.

He had to believe that they could still be alive somewhere, although he couldn't imagine where they could have hidden. At any rate, there was no use standing there with the hungry baby and nothing but smoke all around. Joseph began to walk, not knowing which way to go, simply hoping that there was somewhere left in the world that was better than this.

It must have been difficult for him to feel as if he was making any progress in a world that seemed to have been violently robbed of all its landmarks. Florence's cries were growing more and more feeble; the baby needed to be fed, but there didn't seem to be anything even vaguely edible anywhere that Joseph looked. He kept on walking, up and down the blackened hills, his ruined shoes soon covered in soot, ankles aching as they twisted on the scorched unevenness of the ground.

At last, among the blackness, Joseph saw something stirring. He hurried forward. It was a cow—one of Wisconsin's treasured dairy cows. Her coat smelled of burned hair, and she'd been burned herself in the fire but not fatally so. Like him and Florence, she was wandering across the empty landscape, lost and hurting.

Joseph realized that her udder was full. Somehow, he'd come across a lactating dairy cow, and she was docile enough to stand still as he hurried up to her. He wiped his hands as clean as he could on his coat and set Florence down in her basket before hunkering down beside the cow and grasping one of her teats. Wonderfully, a great jet of white milk squirted warmly onto his palm. Joseph grabbed the baby and held his trembling hand to her lips. As soon as she tasted the milk, she began to drink, and Joseph milked out handful after handful until little Florence's thirst was more or less quenched at last.

The baby went to sleep, but Joseph couldn't find the same peace as he tucked her back into her basket. There was still no sign at all of the Villers. He had no reason to believe that they could still be alive, he realized.

Joseph had already been orphaned once before in his life. Holding the baby, staring out at a desolate world underneath a sun darkened by smoke, the boy realized that Florence might very well now share his fate.

* * * *

Father Pernin could see nothing. He was terrified to move, well aware of the flames and hazards all around him, but equally petrified to stay where he was. He began to stumble around, slowly and carefully, his hands outstretched, as he tried to keep away from the two hazards he could hear: the snapping fires that still burned all around him and the rush of the river beside him.

He was truly blind now, and he felt alone and very vulnerable among the dangers surrounding him. It was a blessed relief when he heard a friendly voice calling his name. Stopping, Father Pernin held out his hands toward the voice. Two hands gripped his own; they felt warm and alive and real and whole. He could have wept for relief if his eyes had been working. The voice told him to come somewhere safe, and Father Pernin clung to the hand that had been offered to him and followed it willingly wherever it led.

All around, he could still feel odd flashes of heat when they passed by a fire. His feet were crunching on ruins, and the smell of smoke assailed his nostrils, choking his already burning lungs. Walking was still difficult, but he kept going as well as he could, hoping for the promise of sanctuary.

And it seemed that he was being led to safety at last. The smell of smoke gave way to something crisp, something fresher. The sound of the fire receded behind him, and something soft was brushing against him. When he reached out to touch it, Father Pernin realized that it was a tree branch covered in leaves. He'd been taken somewhere that had been untouched by the fire. Later, the priest would realize that this was the very river valley where he had hoped to find shelter when he first left his little home by the saloon. The saloon itself had been utterly demolished —two hundred people had died within it when the fire approached and devoured it in a matter of minutes. The low-lying little valley had been protected, as the firestorm had moved so fast that it passed right over the top without touching down within.

Father Pernin could hear voices now too, people talking, people who had survived. It was an inexpressible relief after the aching loneliness of the riverbank. Then, an appalling sound rose from among the reassuring chatter. It was the shrill, desperate cry of someone in mortal pain.

Goosebumps rose on Father Pernin's neck as he struggled to see. He was being led right toward a woman who had been burned beyond recognition yet somehow was still alive. Her skin looked as though it had melted right off her, leaving broken and charred flesh behind. She had been too weak to stand in the river, but even on the very bank of the water, she'd burned almost to death.

As a priest, Father Pernin had ministered to many dying people, and he knew that this poor woman was on death's very door. Normally, he would be beginning the last rites now, administering the Blessed Sacrament to this dying woman for the very last time. But the Eucharist was lost somewhere in the tabernacle, burned for all he knew, or perhaps swept away by the river. Father Pernin's heart ached. He bent down beside the woman, trying to find a part of her to touch that wouldn't result in terrible agony, and he did his best to comfort her as well as he could. It wasn't much; he could barely speak at all, and his eyes could hardly open. Her terrible cries began to fade, and at last, she died.

It was now truly day, and the world had begun to realize that something awful had happened in Peshtigo. Apart from Peshtigo and Sugar Bush, many of the nearby towns had suffered comparatively little. The people were starving after hours spent fleeing the blaze or submerged in the river. Father Pernin could offer little except words of consolation, telling them that people would come from Marinette and that they could shelter in the church, schoolhouse, and presbytery that had just been built there. A few men went scavenging for food, returning only with some raw cabbages that they'd found in a field. It was a wonderful thing when help began to arrive later that afternoon.

William Ogden's company had sent a tent to serve as shelter for the injured. A few hours later, the people from Father Pernin's other parish, Marinette, arrived with cartloads of coffee, tea, and bread. Father Pernin was utterly delighted to hear them coming. He'd begun to wonder if they'd been consumed by the fire just like Peshtigo, but here they were, thrusting hot beverages and soft buns into his hands. Before he could eat, the priest had to find out what had happened in the village. He grasped at one of the men who'd come with the food and asked him what had happened in Marinette.

The man's news was positive. No one had died; the destruction did not approach the same devastating scale as in Peshtigo, but many homes had been lost.

"And the church?" Father Pernin cried.

The man told him that it had been burned. The priest's heart sank. He'd lost both of his churches in a single night. He asked after the new presbytery that he was supposed to have moved into within a few weeks.

"Burned," said the man.

Father Pernin realized that he was now homeless. "The new schoolhouse?" he whispered through his chapped and raw lips.

"Burned also," said the man.

Father Pernin realized, thunderstruck, that he had survived that terrible night, but nothing he owned, and none of the building he'd worked so hard to build for his parishioners, had made it through the night with him. He'd lost everything, and he had nowhere to take his parishioners now.

Nowhere at all.

* * * *

Amelia Desrochers was very quiet as she walked hand in hand with her mother, staring at what had become of the woods that were once her home. Only the river, its waters murky and muddied with debris, was more or less recognizable as her family headed back to the farm where they'd lived just 24 hours ago. The banks were charred, stripped of trees, the earth laid bare by the ravages of the flames.

There were sights there that no five-year-old child should ever have seen, but there was no protecting Amelia from what had happened. She stared at the burned carcasses of the wild animals who'd been too slow to flee from the danger, at the charred relics of the bridge. And after a few minutes' walking, they came upon the bodies.

The town's dam had been opened to drain the river enough for people to start pulling dead bodies out of the water, and there were so many of them. They'd been swept away in the current, crushed by debris floating down the river, trampled by panicked animals, or succumbed to the creeping killer of hypothermia. Men everywhere were pulling corpses out of the water, laying them out on blankets on the riverbank. They were unrecognizable now and frightening to the little girl; their faces were mottled and puffy, their eyes glassy, open. She thought of the people she'd seen jumping off the barge in terror when it caught fire. Many of them had drowned and lay here in the brutal, shaded sunlight, dead.

Among them was a baby, surrounded only by the coldness of the dead. It was still very much alive, and its thin, reedy cry rose into the desolate woods. The sight of it struck so deeply into Amelia's heart that she would never forget it. It was a terrible brand on her memory, one that would remain with her to her dying day.

* * * *

For three long days, three days that must have felt like an eternity, Joseph wandered through the wasteland of the wilderness, his arms wrapped around little Florence. Somehow, the cow must have survived, for so did the baby; Joseph managed to feed and care for her as he continued to search for his adoptive parents.

But after three days alone in the blasted wilderness with a baby to care for, one can only imagine that fourteen-year-old Joseph was beginning to lose hope.

It's not clear exactly how it happened. Whether he eventually managed to find his way to Peshtigo or whether they were the ones who went looking for him, we will never know. But we do know that somehow, on another cold gray day after the fire, Joseph turned around to see Martin and Octavia calling for him.

They had somehow survived the blaze too, and they'd been searching for Joseph and their baby. And when they saw him and saw that he was holding an unhurt and healthy little Florence, they were overjoyed.

Joseph's ordeal was over at last. He ran to his adoptive parents, throwing himself into their arms and holding out their baby girl to them. Octavia pulled little Florence close to her, overcome with relief. For three days, she and Martin had feared the worst. Yet, thanks to little Joseph's courage, Florence was alive and well.

So many of Peshtigo's residents had died in the consuming flames. Those who survived counted themselves lucky. But their ordeal was a long way from over.

Chapter 7 – Flickers of Hope

Illustration IV: The Peshtigo Fire Cemetery

When the night receded, taking the fire with it, Abram Place was half astonished to discover that all of his efforts had been worth it. Together with the help of the Ojibwe, he had somehow managed to save his home. It was sodden with their efforts, and they were all exhausted, but it had been worth it. All around Abram's home, the woods had been reduced to a great black scar upon the earth. But his house still stood. Abram and his family were safe.

The Ojibwe said their goodbyes and melted back into the woods. They, too, must have suffered in the blaze, but the effect on their population was never recorded. Still, it's doubtless that the Place's farm could never have survived without their help.

Pariah though Abram was, it wasn't long before the people of Peshtigo began to notice that the wealthy farmer's house and barn were still standing. This was one of the only buildings that were left at all in the whole area, and so, people began to come to him, carrying their wounded, their eyes grieved. Only days ago, they'd seen Abram as a nobody, a blight on the face of their society. Now, for many, he was their only hope. Abram and his Ojibwe wife threw their doors wide to welcome the people; in the days that followed, their home would be transformed into a field hospital to treat the many victims of the fire.

* * * *

Father Pernin was not one of the wounded who ended up being taken to the field hospital at Abram Place's farm. Instead, his parishioners brought the injured priest back to Marinette, where he was delivered into the compassion and care of one of his Marinette parishioners.

The priest had lost everything, and now, he was in danger of losing both his eyesight and even his life. Smoke inhalation is an insidious killer, and burns can also be easily infected. After having spent hours in the most disgusting of conditions, Father Pernin was at great risk of both. However, his parishioner took excellent care of him, and after just two days, he bounced back. He was able to walk around once more, and he immediately asked to be taken to Peshtigo on the Tuesday afternoon after the blaze. He needed to see what had become of his people there.

The sight that greeted him was a terrible one. Many parts of Marinette had been burned, but it was at least still recognizable as a town. Peshtigo looked like a battlefield. More than that—it looked like it had been purposefully destroyed done to every last brick, as every last building has been reduced to nothing but coals.

First, Father Pernin asked to be taken to his church or what was left of it. If the fire had never come through Peshtigo, then that church would be freshly plastered. Perhaps he would even have been thinking about holding a mass there the following Sunday for the first time. Instead, he was picking his way through the rubble, months of hard work reduced to dust. The strangest sight was a molten pool of what had once been metal. It was all that remained of the church's bell. Father Pernin's heart squeezed as he thought of the tabernacle he had abandoned.

This was nowhere near to the worst sight that greeted him on that awful day. The streets he'd once loved were now littered with corpses; most of them were charred utterly beyond recognition, so much so that hundreds of them would be buried in a mass grave all together, never identified thanks to how badly they'd been burned. People had been reduced to little heaps of ash. Others were horribly bloated by the water as people began to bring up the drowned from the riverbed. Yet others looked strangely peaceful and untouched; they had died of cold after escaping the heat.

And most tragic of all, there were those who had slit their own throats and killed their own children in order to spare them the horrendous death of burning alive. They found whole families together who had committed suicide in the face of the oncoming wall of fire. Father Pernin remembered the people on the riverbank who, despairing of any hope of survival, had stopped and allowed the flames to come for them when they were just a few steps away from the water. He wondered how many of them he had not been able to save.

Father Pernin himself was still weak and unwell, but he knew that his people needed him. Even though he still lacked any of the things he needed to administer the last rites, since his church at Marinette had been burned to the ground as well, he began to move among the wounded and dying, offering prayers and consolation wherever he could. It felt small and futile in the face of the disaster, but perhaps, he hoped, it would comfort a few people.

He was busy caring for those whom he could help when one of his parishioners ran up to him with shining eyes. "Father!" he said. "Do you know what's happened to your tabernacle?"

For all he knew, the tabernacle was also nothing but ash now too. "No," said Father Pernin. "What is it?"

The man was wildly excited. "Come quickly and see!"

Father Pernin hurried after the parishioner as well as he could and was greeted with a surprising sight. The tabernacle he'd risked his life to save had not been lost to the fire or the water after all. The wagon had toppled over, its remnants jutting out of the river, but the white wooden box of the tabernacle itself had landed on one of the logs that had been floating on the river. Somehow, the wind must have swept it over there—it had definitely been strong enough to do. And although parts of the log were charred, the tabernacle was utterly unharmed.

Perhaps the sight of that little white box sparked the first flicker of hope felt in a Peshtigo resident's heart for days and days. And as the days passed, and the citizens began to try to comprehend what their lives would be now that everything they had was destroyed, they would need all the hope they could get.

Almost immediately, the people of Peshtigo began to run into problems as they sought help from their fellow Americans. The first was that there was simply no way to get word to the rest of the world. As far as most Americans were concerned, life was going on as usual in Peshtigo. The telegraph poles had long since been destroyed in the flames, so it was only when a man on horseback managed to make his way down the treacherous road to Green Bay, which was blocked by many fallen trees and smoldering fires, that a telegram could be sent to Chicago. It was simple and heart-wrenching. "We are burning up. Send help."

That was when the residents of Peshtigo realized that their life had become much more complicated already. For on the very night that Peshtigo faced a firestorm, Chicago itself was being burned down. Governor Lucius Fairchild already had his hands full trying to provide aid to the city, which had suffered devastating losses, when word reached him of the plight of Peshtigo.

And Peshtigo's plight was a terrible one indeed. Twelve hundred people had died in Peshtigo alone—two-thirds of its population wiped out, horribly killed, in a single night. Counting the deaths in Sugar Bush and other towns, as many as 2,500 people may have perished that day. It's hard to tell, though, because so many of the town's records were also destroyed in the fire.

Nearly two thousand acres of the woods and farms had been destroyed in the blaze as well. Not only were hundreds of people left without homes, but the very lifeblood of Peshtigo—its lumber—had been decimated. The total loss in terms of money was around $169 million, equal in today's money to more than $3 billion.

Chicago had suffered roughly the same loss, and Governor Fairchild was dismayed when he heard of what had happened in Peshtigo. But the facts remained the same: he would have to provide aid to the smaller town as well. A train of supplies was already heading north to Chicago, and when Fairchild's wife, Frances, heard of the Peshtigo fire, she rerouted a boxcar to head as far up the railroad as it could in that direction. It wasn't much, but it was enough to keep the citizens alive while Frances Fairchild got to work. She initiated a blanket drive in the city of Madison and began to coordinate various relief efforts, including involving the US military.

The army was, in the end, one of the greatest saviors of Peshtigo. Huge donations poured to the city, including 4,000 blankets, over 1,500 outfits, and 200,000 basic rations of food. Peshtigo residents finally had almost everything they needed to get through the winter.

When the cold descended, the people at least had some shelter and enough food and clothes for the winter. But as it turned out, winter was one thing. Spring was entirely another.

The usual glorious green that came over the Wisconsin woods when the snow receded was sadly absent in 1872. The effects of the fire went even deeper than the undergrowth and trees that it had burned away. The soil had been badly affected by the fire, its layer of undergrowth burned away, soot and ash affecting its balance. To make matters even worse, what little crops the townsfolk could coax out of the wounded earth were destroyed when a great plague of army bugs—better known as stink bugs today—descended on the area. The swarms of insects chewed up every green thing that managed to grow.

As if that wasn't bad enough, the bugs were followed by a cloud of parasitic flies. These preyed on the army bugs, which at least caused a reduction in their numbers, but the flies also swarmed all over the town, buzzing in the crisp spring air and filling the sky as the smoke had done on that fateful October night. It was as if all of nature had risen up in arms to expel the hapless residents from the woods.

In the end, many of the farmers and lumberjacks of Peshtigo realized that there was no way they could stay there. The area had become almost uninhabitable. In a bid to help, the US government provided each family of Peshtigo with $50 and free transport to anywhere they wanted to go in the country. The cash would be worth around $1,000 in today's money, and it was enough for families to make a fresh start somewhere a long way away from the blighted town.

After that terrible night on the raft, Lars Korstad was one of the people who jumped at the chance to leave Peshtigo behind for greener pastures, or at least somewhere that wasn't being plagued like biblical Egypt. He wanted Anna to grow up somewhere green and happy, where there was hope and joy and not the desolation he saw in the eyes of the other townsfolk. At first, Lars wanted to take her and his wife to California; the Gold Rush had opened up the way for pioneering families to make their fortunes out there. In the end, though, he didn't leave Wisconsin. He moved his family to the nearby city of LaCrosse, where Anna grew up. She eventually married, becoming Mrs. Anna Iverson, and lived for a long time to tell the tale of her courageous parents and how they'd saved her from the very midst of the firestorm.

The Desrochers family, however, chose to stay in Peshtigo. They were pioneers at heart, and even though their dreams had been reduced to ashes around them, something called them to stay—history has forgotten what exactly. For whatever reason, the Desrochers family hung on with incredible tenacity, rebuilding their lives despite the fire, the bugs, and the flies, allowing Amelia to grow up watching Peshtigo rise from the ashes.

Even when Amelia became an adult, and even though the trauma of that fire still haunted her as she heard the cries of that lonely baby every time she walked past that particular piece of riverbank, she never left Peshtigo for long. She made a life for herself there with the people she loved. Among them was Wesley Duket, a fellow survivor of the fire. Details of the blaze would stay with Wesley for the rest of his life too: the panicked crashing of a shed full of young horses as they burned in his family's barn, his sister saving her sewing machine by wrapping it in a quilt, the body of his beloved neighbor, Mrs. Reinhart, burned to death. Only a scrap of her shawl remained—a scrap that Wesley would carry in his pocket for years after the event. He didn't need the reminder. The trauma of that day would stay with him forever.

Amelia was similarly scarred, and yet she stayed in the city that rebuilt itself slowly over the following decades, refusing to relinquish whatever was left of its pioneering spirit despite all that it had endured. Amelia and Wesley became close friends for life. Eventually, they both ended up in the same retirement home, and they spent hours together in peaceful reminiscence as they gazed out upon a rebuilt Peshtigo. She died at a good old age.

As for Joseph LaCrosse, the rest of the young orphan's life has been lost to time after his heroic rescue of baby Florence and his reunion with Martin and Octavia. He faded into history as if he was of little consequence—except he did matter, and his courageous acts live on in the descendants of the baby he rescued from the blaze. Little Florence grew up, and in time, she married a man named Eli Cayemberg. They would go on to be a happy—and definitely fertile—couple: today, there are more than five hundred descendants of Florence Cayemberg.

History may have forgotten Joseph, but Florence's descendants never did. Decades after the fire, they erected a memorial stone to the brave orphan, knowing that if he hadn't thought to pick up that baby and climb into that well in the face of certain death, none of them would be alive today. The stone still stands in Peshtigo as a silent testimony to the power of a single person's compassion and courage.

* * * *

As for Father Pernin, he, too, tried his best to cling to Peshtigo for as long as he could but to no avail.

The bishop of the area, Bishop Joseph Melcher, lived in Green Bay, and he was appalled when the early news of Peshtigo reached him, telling him that one of his most active and vigorous priests, Peter Pernin, was dead. The poor bishop could hardly believe his eyes when he opened his front door one morning, about a week after the fire, only to find himself nose to nose with an apparent specter: a scarred, red-eyed, and sickly Father Pernin. Once he'd gotten over his initial shock, Bishop Melcher was quick to usher Father Pernin into his home, overjoyed to see that the priest had survived the blaze.

It was an exhausted and battered version of the priest he'd known before the fire, though. The Father Pernin of a few weeks ago had been a sprightly, busy character, never stopping and talking of his plans to build churches and schools and presbyteries in two different parishes. This one was sadly beaten by all that he had experienced. Father Pernin's sight had returned in full, but his muscular frame had been shrunken by trauma, and he moved gingerly and in pain. Bishop Melcher's heart went out to his younger friend. He offered at once for Father Pernin to be transferred to a different parish, a prosperous, established settlement some ways away, perhaps, where he wouldn't have so much to do.

Father Pernin regarded the offer soberly for some time. It was certainly very appealing. The work of a parish priest could be a heart-wrenching one in a time such as this. He would have to try to make sense of all this to people who thought they'd just seen the world end. There were so many families with great holes torn in them. So many people suffering trauma and grief, people with hard and aching questions, and they would turn to him for answers. What was more, people weren't finished dying from the Peshtigo fire. Many were still suffering from burns and smoke inhalation; sadly, many of these would die within the next few months when infections took their toll.

Father Pernin had already seen so many people die. Moving to a different settlement, where he just had to go through the motions of mass and other rituals, would suit him well. Father Pernin was himself suffering mentally after what he'd seen and experienced.

But he couldn't bring himself to take Bishop Melcher's offer. His people needed him. In his own words, he thought, "How much better it was that their poverty and privations should be shared by one who knew and loved them." Father Pernin couldn't bear to see Peshtigo left without a priest or, perhaps even worse, in the hands of some stranger who didn't understand what those people had just gone through. He could leave, but many of his parishioners couldn't. Abandoning them was unthinkable. He begged for permission to stay with his parish, and, reluctantly, Bishop Melcher gave it.

It was a noble thing to do but an unwise one. Father Pernin would have been better off taking Bishop Melcher's advice. Over the next few weeks, faced over and over again by the appalling reality of what had happened in Peshtigo, Father Pernin's mental and physical health both began to fail. His thoughts grew scrambled, darkened by the terrible stain of trauma, and his once-powerful frame—one that had pulled a buggy like a horse—turned weak and wasted. When the parish priest of Green Bay approached Father Pernin to preach for him on All Saints' Day just three weeks after the fire, he found that the priest had been reduced to a shadow of the powerful and vigorous man he once used to be. Father Pernin's speech was messy; his thoughts even more so. The Green Bay priest was left to conclude that his unfortunate colleague had suffered brain damage after the tragedy he'd been through. He spoke to Bishop Melcher, who, in turn, convinced Father Pernin that he really did need to get away from Peshtigo.

Father Pernin relented. He would travel to Louisiana, he thought, and find some recuperation in a warmer and more civilized part of the United States. But his health was so poor that even that trip proved impossible. He only made it as far as St. Louis, Missouri, before fever struck him down in his tracks. The citizens of the town were generous in caring for the fallen man of God, but it was clear that he could go no farther. He stayed there to recuperate.

Somehow, months later, Father Pernin did recover. And once he could, he did what he'd wanted to do in the first place: he returned to the stricken towns of Marinette and Peshtigo.

There, he was presented with a new problem. The church of Marinette was ready to be rebuilt, but there were no funds to rebuild it. Everything that Father Pernin himself had owned had been destroyed in the fire; the community was impoverished, the landscape ravaged by the flames, and the people were barely surviving in Wisconsin. But across the United States, people were practically oblivious of what had happened. Father Pernin realized that he had something he could offer the world, something that would help to bring money in: his words. And so, the priest set pen to paper and composed his book, *The Finger of God is There*, now better known as *The Great Fire of Peshtigo: An Eyewitness Account*. It was published in 1874, and it remains a breathtakingly vivid account of what really happened that night. Father Pernin did not merely tell his story. He bled it onto the page.

The church at Peshtigo was rebuilt and eventually converted into a museum, which is still open today. Marinette's church, too, was rebuilt, and Father Pernin would serve there as a priest until 1876. From there, he would spend the rest of his life ministering to one town or the other, usually in Wisconsin, but occasionally in Minnesota. After 1898, when he was serving in the town of Rushford, he fades from the records, but his fearless words live on.

As for the tabernacle of the Peshtigo church, the one that had been saved from the blaze by a timely gust of wind, it disappeared sometime during Father Pernin's lifetime. For decades, its location remained a total mystery. It was more than a hundred years later that the tabernacle was located at last and identified as being the very same one that had nearly been washed away in the river that night. Today, it is in Peshtigo itself. For most of the year, it resides at St. Mary's Church in Peshtigo (not far from Father Pernin's home and the original church), where it still remains a symbol of hope to Catholics. And in the summer, it is displayed at the Peshtigo Fire Museum as a symbol of survival to everyone.

Chapter 8 – Composed of Wind and Fire

Illustration V: A firestorm in the Mirror Plateau

The people of Peshtigo were not unfamiliar with wildfires. In a vast wilderness covered with trees, forest fires were a regrettable fact of life, a regular scourge that the people had to deal with every dry season. But the Great Peshtigo Fire of 1871 was something utterly unprecedented. No one could have even hoped to prepare for it, as no one had ever seen anything like it before.

It wasn't simply the fire's size and speed that made it distinctive, nor the fact that it took so many lives. It was the strange things that they saw.

The strangest of all, of course, was the pillar of fire that many of them noted approaching them right before the great tragedy. But there were other things, too, things that didn't make sense. Father Pernin recorded many of these, listening patiently to frightened survivors as they recounted their tales. He would hardly have believed them if he hadn't lived through it himself. They spoke of whole maple trees, not burned away but simply ripped out of the ground by the roots as if torn up by a giant hand as easily as a gardener pulls a weed. Those giant trees were thrown to the ground in great swathes.

Others reported seeing entire wooden houses lifted clean from their foundations and thrown into the air, where they spun wildly before being consumed entirely by the flames, their pieces scattered everywhere by the wind. Father Pernin himself saw how completely the flame could devour something as sturdy and mighty as a great tree, for he came upon a place where the very roots had been burned right down into the ground. The priest had thrust his stick down into the blackened holes as far as he could. The roots were gone except for a little ash, as the fire had consumed the entire tree, both above and below ground.

Father Pernin had already come across his melted church bell, but there was more evidence all around Peshtigo that the fire had been unbelievably hot. Whole hogsheads full of nails had been melted into a pool of hot iron, and charred corpses could not even be identified by their pocket watches because the latter had been reduced to blobs of unrecognizable metal.

Of course, hundreds of land-dwelling animals had died, but even birds and fish had not been able to flee from the wrath of the fire. Survivors spoke of birds being sucked into the flames by the wind or even catching fire where they flew, the embers lighting on their feathers and setting them ablaze mid-flight.

The fate of the fish was perhaps the strangest of all. Many kinds of fish of all different sizes had died in the river itself; the next morning, they were floating all over the surface, a macabre collection of shiny sides, white bellies, damp fins, and staring eyes.

There were many things that the survivors told of and that their contemporaries recorded that just didn't add up for many years. In fact, for decades, it was tempting to dismiss many of the strange things that were recorded about the Great Fire of Peshtigo to be nothing but the hysterical figments of imaginations tortured by trauma and terror.

Almost 150 years later, we know better. We know that what the people saw that night was not a result of hysteria. It was something very terrifying, very rare, and very real, something that would result in the same type of fear and panic in the modern day. The dreadful testimonies of those wild-eyed survivors might sound like fiction, but they are backed by science.

The strange phenomena had led Father Pernin and many others, including the scientists of the day, to conclude that the Great Fire of Peshtigo had occurred in the presence of some kind of flammable gas. Many speculated that swamp gas had risen into the air, caught fire, and then burned in the air itself. Father Pernin had seen a whole sky transfixed by flame. It had certainly felt as though the air he breathed was itself afire. This theory may sound credible, but it's highly unlikely that this was the case.

However, when recording the survivors' tales, Father Pernin did stumble upon the real secret as to why the Great Fire of Peshtigo had turned so tremendously savage. He himself had touched upon the terrifying truth, even though he didn't know it, when he called it a "hurricane, seemingly composed of wind and fire together."

Many of the survivors to whom Father Pernin spoke described something that the priest could not begin to make sense of, let alone understand, but there were so many people that were so thoroughly convinced of what they'd seen that he could not ignore it. He recorded the phenomenon in his book, albeit sounding dubious about whether or not the vision he described had really occurred. These eyewitness accounts confirm what science already knows.

The people had spoken of a great, terrible, floating object that had been in the sky as the storm came upon them. They described it as dark, black, or balloon-like. Everything it touched seemed to burst instantly into flame; sometimes, it would pass by whole stands of trees or even homes without causing any damage, then set a line of the forest alight in one touch. They also said that it had revolved, spinning with enormous speed above the woods like some great dancing demon of death.

The people had not seen a demon, but they had seen something that would strike fear into even the most courageous heart. They'd witnessed a tornado made of fire.

* * * *

The science of the Great Fire of Peshtigo is simple enough to understand, even though its scale and destruction are difficult to comprehend.

It doesn't take any kind of a scientist to imagine how the fire itself had begun. A drought had left those woods tinder-dry, and when farmers and lumberjacks continued to use slash-and-burn methods to clear their lands, they unwittingly caused a huge number of small fires to start up all over those Wisconsin woods. There is no way to pinpoint the single origin of the Great Fire of Peshtigo because there was no single origin. It was the result of many cumulative factors, and at the end of the day, all those little fires came together and roared up into the breathtaking force of nature that the fire became.

Gusting winds combining with dry conditions made everything much, much worse. A huge cell of low pressure came over the area at the time, causing incredible winds. In fact, such cells, when combined with rain, can turn into hurricanes, and this cell was a similar situation, but it was too dry to cause a storm of that nature. Instead, it simply caused huge amounts of wind, and those winds fanned the little fires into ferocity.

To make matters even worse, it was recently discovered that even small fires can behave in unpredictable and frightening ways when faced with winds of that magnitude. Normal wildfires behave in a fairly logical manner: fires move downwind. If the wind blows in a fairly constant direction, small fires can be isolated and dealt with. But when the wind blows hard enough in a hilly country, the results can be catastrophic. A fire racing uphill with the wind can suddenly change direction as a result of wind eddies. When the wind is moving too fast to blow back down the hill, it blows across the top instead, creating a vacuum that sucks air down and against itself, blowing the fire back on itself. Having nowhere else to go, the fire is forced sideways, becoming a crosswind instead of going downwind. This incredibly unpredictable phenomenon can cause fires to rush in apparently illogical directions, and it can cause small fires to connect with larger fires at incredible speed. An entire hill could be ablaze in seconds as a result of this phenomenon. Thus, it didn't take long before all the little fires set by those clearing brush for farming or logging to be whipped together into one enormous blaze.

When a fire first begins, it is driven by the weather. But should a fire grow to great enough proportions, it no longer relies on the weather; in fact, it begins to affect the immediate climate, manipulating the conditions that gave birth to it. This began to occur in Peshtigo when the fire grew to a massive size.

To understand this phenomenon, it's time to look at some basic chemistry. Fires are a byproduct of combustion, which is a chemical reaction. In this reaction, oxygen in the air reacts with organic compounds, which contain carbon and hydrogen. (This is why fires need both air and fuel to survive.) The reaction releases large amounts of energy in the form of heat, which we see as flames, but it also creates products in the form of carbon dioxide and water. The water, of course, is in its gaseous form as water vapor due to the intense heat.

Now, back to basic physics. When any substance is cooled, the molecules lose energy, causing them to stay closer together, resulting in increased density. Cold air is denser than hot air. Thus, hot air will rise above cold air, just like oil rises above water. Of course, the huge fire began to heat the air surrounding it, which caused that hot air to rise up into the atmosphere. The hot air carried lighter particles with it: water vapor, smoke, and ash.

As these particles continued to rise and rise, accumulating as more and more of them were produced and the hot air kept blowing up into the atmosphere, they began to form something extraordinary: a cloud. Clouds formed by fire are called pyroclouds. Many fires can form pyrocumulus clouds, which are harmless but impressive to look at. But on that dark fall evening of 1871, the massive cloud that formed above the raging flames was much more than that. It was a pyrocumulonimbus cloud, a thundercloud created by fire. These enormous clouds can extend more than nine miles up into the sky, reaching even the stratosphere itself. And thus, a storm is born of fire.

This phenomenon, known as a firestorm, is defined as a thunderstorm with its own wind system that is generated by a wildfire. A big enough fire can actually create its own weather, such as a storm, where there was nothing before. It can even cause dry lightning. Cruelly, the town of Peshtigo had seen no storms all summer. The pyrocumulonimbus cloud that formed over the woods that day was the first cloud the people there had seen for months. Did they hope that the storm would bring rain and that the rain would put out the fire?

Tragically, nothing could be further from the truth. The firestorm only made matters a thousand times worse.

Thanks to the constant movement of air—remember that hot air rises into the atmosphere and cools, causing it to come back down as more hot air rises, a process known as convection—firestorms can generate their own winds, and as the people of Peshtigo were about to experience, those winds can be utterly devastating. When Father Pernin's housemaid felt her canary's cage being ripped out of her very hands, it was likely from a powerful gust of wind originating from the firestorm itself. These gusts of wind are some of the most dangerous phenomena that a firestorm can produce. They're known as downbursts: great, vertical thrusts of wind that rush to the ground, strike it with enormous force, and then scatter, sending bursts of wind in every direction. When downbursts occur into a fire, the results are truly disastrous, as fires become completely unpredictable.

A firestorm can be devastating enough. The residents of Peshtigo were in trouble either way, but what they experienced next was something that had never been recorded before, something that the world has seldom seen. It is the rarest and most dangerous phenomenon that can be created by a fire: a fire tornado.

Any large enough thunderstorm can create the right conditions for a tornado, and a firestorm is no exception. In fact, most firestorms create little mini-tornadoes, small columns of spinning flames called fire whirls. These are short-lived, small in scale, and don't move very fast. While fire whirls can be devastating enough, they're puny compared to what happened at Peshtigo on the night of October 8th, 1871.

That night, the firestorm created a convection column, a tunnel of rotating air formed by the rise and fall of hot and cold air. Only this time, the column was not made of wind and rain like it would be in a tornado. It was made of wind and flames, and it moved at great speed. It is characterized as a fire tornado as opposed to a fire whirl partly because of the fact that the whole thing could lift up into the air, clearing the ground completely. The survivors that spoke of how the tornado seemed to choose certain areas for destruction and leave others untouched are proof of this, as well as Father Pernin's observation that the low-lying areas appeared to be the least affected by the blaze.

Fire tornadoes are impossible to control, even today. There was nothing that the people of Peshtigo could have done to stop it and very little that they could have done to escape it. Fire tornadoes have a savage strength; they have been recorded as snapping trees in half, tearing roofs off houses, and throwing cars into the air, just like a normal tornado. Those survivors that told Father Pernin they'd seen houses torn off their foundations and thrown into the sky weren't crazy after all. In a fire tornado of that magnitude, it really could have happened. The people who saw a big black balloon spinning in the sky were really seeing the top of the tornado; the blackness was caused by the smoke.

Of course, Father Pernin didn't get to see the firenado from a distance, as his view was blocked by trees and buildings. Instead, the priest and those near him were trapped in the belly of the firenado itself.

Faced with these awe-inspiring forces of nature, it's truly amazing that anyone in Peshtigo survived at all, and it is hardly surprising that the whole settlement of Sugar Bush was so completely and effectively wiped out in a single night. Today, firestorms and fire tornadoes still happen, although the latter are very rare due to the specific conditions required to form them. They still can't be controlled, and they still destroy many homes and farms, as they have done for centuries.

Chapter 9 – Wildfires through American History

Even before Europeans ever set foot in the United States, wildfires had been a natural occurrence and a fact of life for centuries. It's thought that Native Americans may have even used fire as a tool to clear land, fight enemies, and manage the wilderness that had been their home for generations. We have no real record of fires before the 19th century, but the stories we can tell about the blazes that have raged since are as chilling as they are filled with heroism.

The Great Peshtigo Fire was the deadliest wildfire in American history, but even today, its occurrence was eclipsed by one simple fact—the Great Chicago Fire occurred on the very same night. This fire was less deadly, but it was far more publicized, leading to its place being well secured in history, while the devastation at Peshtigo received far less attention in the press.

The Great Chicago Fire is still one of the most famous in American history, and perhaps part of this is due to the neat little myth that comes along with it. A myth that caused one family an endless amount of pain and hardship.

* * * *

Catherine O'Leary could hardly believe her eyes.

When she'd heard the knock on her door, she'd been wary. The past few weeks had taught her that the world was a much less hospitable place than she'd thought, and Catherine had already felt the brunt of the world's cruelty. She had immigrated to Chicago from an Ireland racked by famine, and she was just scrambling to keep her head above water in her home in the southwest of the city, along with her husband and five children. But ever since those awful two days in October, Catherine had become the scapegoat for a tragedy that had killed hundreds. She had faced so many reporters that she hardly knew what to do with herself.

But this...this was something else.

She stared at the jovial, round-cheeked man with his receding hairline of thick, dark curls and bright eyes, and had to blink several times to make sure she wasn't dreaming. She wasn't. She was looking at P. T. Barnum, the owner of America's first traveling circus, and he was looking at her with sparkling eyes. As soon as he spoke, the reason for his strange visit was unmistakable. He wanted Catherine O'Leary for his circus. He wanted to showcase her alongside his famous Fiji mermaid and the two-foot-tall General Tom Thumb because she had become, in his eyes, a sensation like them: a creature that would arouse the mingled curiosity and horror upon which he'd built his empire. Catherine could picture herself posing for wide-eyed crowds of peanut-chomping children as the woman who'd burned down Chicago.

Catherine had had quite enough. Seizing a broomstick, she chased the man from her home, furious.

Catherine's life had changed on October 8th, 1871, the very same night that all of Peshtigo was wrapped in a tornado of flame. That was the night that another fire began, a fire that would cause the destruction of one of America's fastest-growing cities. Chicago burned the same night that Peshtigo did, and Catherine's memories of that awful time were fresh with trauma. Her husband had shaken her awake in horror late that evening. "Cate, the barn is afire!" he'd cried. She ran outside, but it was already too late. The barn containing their five dairy cows—her only means of making a living—was already enveloped in flames.

Somehow, the O'Leary family's home was spared, and so was 44-year-old Catherine and her family. Her losses had been great, but they could have been much greater. Catherine was grateful—until the first papers came out, telling the story that has become a legend. Her cow had kicked over a lantern, setting her barn alight and starting the fire. Catherine was officially to blame, even though all the evidence would point to her being completely innocent. The story likely originated from neighborhood children or an overly imaginative newspaper.

No matter how the fire originated, Chicago was ripe for the burning. It had suffered from the same drought as Peshtigo, and it was constructed almost entirely of wood. The fire quickly developed into a fully-fledged firestorm itself. While it didn't create the same firenado as Peshtigo's did, it did cause fire whirls even though the winds weren't strong that night, and these ignited block after city block of tinder-dry wooden buildings. Those fire whirls leaped a hundred feet in the air as despairing firemen hurried in an attempt to save the city.

They made a little more progress than the people of Peshtigo had. The city was equipped with fire hydrants, so it was more prepared than the booming little frontier town. Still, they fought that blaze for two long days, and it was only when rain began to fall on October 10th that the fire was finally extinguished. It was two days too long. Three hundred people were dead, another hundred thousand were homeless, and the financial loss was even greater than it had been at Peshtigo.

Catherine had lost her livelihood, but she was also losing her reputation, her friendships, and even her sanity. Despite the fact that setting her barn alight would have been a completely senseless thing to do, the press lapped up the story eagerly. The word "xenophobia" was not yet in common use in 1871, but the concept itself was alive and kicking even then as floods of immigrants swarmed Chicago. An immigrant herself, Catherine made the perfect target for powerful and angry nativists.

She would never escape the blame she didn't deserve. She spent the rest of her life moving around the city, trying to avoid the press until she died 24 years later from pneumonia at the age of 68. The folk songs and myths about her still live on, but in 1997, the city of Chicago formally exonerated her (and her cow) from all blame for starting the fire.

The story of Catherine O'Leary was not the only strange theory that reared its head regarding that October night in 1871. The same night that both Peshtigo and Chicago burned, a series of wildfires exploded across Michigan, claiming over five hundred lives. The fact that so many fires started on the same evening sparked the attention of many scholars. They reasoned that something had to have triggered them all, something more than just the wind and dry conditions. And so, the Biela Comet theory was born.

First proposed in 1883, the Biela Comet theory about the 1871 fires is that the Biela Comet, which had been regularly sighted before the mid-19th century and then mysteriously disappeared, never to be seen again, had disintegrated into a meteor shower that rained burning space rocks onto the dry United States, causing a spree of fires all the way from Illinois to Wisconsin. The theory is intriguing, and it has been explored in numerous modern papers, but it is widely discredited by most physicists. Meteorites are cold by the time they reach the ground. Even if the entire comet had somehow ended up in the atmosphere, it was far more likely to have simply exploded than to shower fire across several states.

Today, the most accepted explanation for the start of the Great Peshtigo Fire is the cumulative effect of dry conditions and poorly regulated fires set by human hands. Still, no one can deny that having three major fires in one night is a truly eerie coincidence.

* * * *

1871 was not the only time that the Great Lakes area would find itself stricken by flame.

Thick woods and constant human expansion regularly resulted in conditions that were favorable for fires. Wildfire season was—and still is—an annual occurrence there, but the next time that the fires grew out of control and started to claim human lives on a terrible scale was in 1881, ten years later. The crude slash-and-burn methods were still being used, and in the September of that year in Michigan's Thumb peninsula, just as it had happened in Peshtigo, massive gales pushed the resulting small fires into an epic firestorm.

The winds were such that they could blow people to the ground and push boulders around, according to some eyewitnesses. By September 4th, the fire had begun in earnest. The sky turned dark around lunchtime that day, the sun a brooding yellow eye glaring down at the world in fevered rage. Before the people of the area could react, the firestorm was right upon them.

Two hundred eighty-two people were killed in the Thumb between September 4th and September 6th. Three thousand four hundred buildings were destroyed, and fifteen thousand people were left homeless.

Eerily, thirteen years later to the very day, on September 4th, 1894, a fire broke out once again in the Great Lakes area. This time, it ravaged the Minnesota side of Lake Superior.

Once again, a dry summer had left the woods ready to be used as tinder. Slash-and-burn was still the preferred method of clearing land, and great piles of useless brush (known as "slash") lay among the trees. Even then, despite the fact that people tried to be cautious enough not to set the slash alight, man-made sparks were still the cause of the fires. By that time, the Great Lakes area was crisscrossed with railroads. Trains had changed transport forever, as they were absolutely invaluable to the people and the economy of the area, and they were far more profuse than in the time of the Great Peshtigo Fire. But they had their downsides, and one of those downsides was that the friction of their iron wheels on iron rails could be severe enough to cause sparks to fly from the rails. Landing on that dry slash, they were more than enough to cause a fire.

This time, the winds were strong enough that the fires became not only a firestorm but another devastating fire tornado. The roaring flames towered four and a half miles into the air. The great glowing column was visible two hundred miles away, and where the tornado passed, it melted the railroads themselves, fusing the wheels of abandoned boxcars to the tracks.

The trains that had caused the fire, ironically, were also one of the only means of salvation for those who rushed to flee from it. Two trains—one for freight, one for passengers—came into the town of Hinckley just as the fire was driving droves of petrified people out of their homes. They emptied their boxcars and brought the people on board as quickly as they could, joining together in order to speed up their flight from the ravaging blaze. Loaded up with hundreds of frightened refugees with sooty faces and terrified eyes, the trains set off as the flames were licking at their heels.

It was a task that would have daunted the bravest of men, and it was a good thing that the engineers of the two trains were some of the bravest there could be. William Barry and Edward Best had set out for another ordinary day on the railroads, but they now found themselves holding hundreds of fragile human fates in their hands as they urged their engines to their best pace through the blazing landscape, leaving a white trail of steam among the roiling black and churning gray and blazing orange of the burning world. They were just beginning to believe that they might outstrip the fire after all when the train began to approach the bridge over the Kettle River. The construction was made largely of timber, and it towered a hundred and fifty feet over the rushing waters below. And when that racing train rushed down upon it, the bridge was already on fire. Flames licked brilliant yellow around its wooden structure.

With flames ahead and flames behind, the engineers were forced to choose between the frying pan and the fire. They both doubted whether the bridge would possibly be able to hold the weight of two engines with fully-loaded boxcars. But to stop and stay on this side of the river would mean nothing but certain death. At least crossing the bridge would give them a chance. Still, it was no task for the fainthearted, and it must have taken a considerable amount of guts to push those engines even faster and race on toward the burning bridge. One can only imagine the shrieks of terror that must have risen up from the packed boxcars when the panicked refugees realized what those engineers were doing. If that bridge buckled beneath the train, it would plummet into the river, and everyone on board would perish.

The train puffed and struggled its way onto the bridge. It shook, and the refugees closed their eyes, and the engineers gritted their teeth, but there was no stopping now. It was an interminably long few moments as the giant train rushed over the blazing bridge. But at last, the horrifying moment was over, and the train had reached the other side with hundreds of living souls that would get to see another day dawn thanks to the courage of William Barry and Edward Best. It was a timely burst of courage, too, with no room for a moment's hesitation: just minutes later, the entire bridge crumbled into charred bits, which fell into the Kettle River and were swept away into oblivion.

The people on the train were all saved. But in Hinckley and its neighboring towns, hundreds of others were not so fortunate. The official death toll of the Great Hinckley Fire of 1894 is 418, but in reality, hundreds more may have perished. As with the Great Fire of Peshtigo, so many records were burned and so many remains left unrecognizable by the flames that it's nearly impossible to tell. Two hundred thousand acres of farmland, woods, and quiet country suburbs were reduced to nothing but soot and ash.

* * * *

On a hot, dry, and windy day in October 1918, a car came squealing down Highway 73 as fast as its driver could push the screaming engine to go. The driver was white-knuckled, white-faced, and clenched-jawed behind the wheel. Smoke blew over the road, leaving his visibility next to nothing, but there was no option of slowing down. On either side of his car, sheets of flame pursued him, licking and spitting at the gleaming flanks of the vehicle like wolves tearing at the sides of a tired deer. The fire was gaining on him. Even though the man had a shining machine of glass and steel at his command, he was fleeing with the same simple, primitive desperation of the animals that scrambled through the woods alongside him. The only thing that mattered was speed and flight.

There was smoke everywhere. The heat of the flames was already penetrating the car, scalding the sides of his face as he drove faster and faster, desperate to escape. And with the smoke lying so thick across his windshield, he never saw the sharp bend in the road coming until it was upon him, and by then, it was already too late. He yanked the wheel hard to the side, stomping on the brake, and the car spun wildly. For a moment, it floated, leaving the road behind, drifting sideways through the air. Then it smacked into the ground. Glass shattered in every direction, and the ruined vehicle tumbled through the woods, its driver killed instantly.

It was October 12th, 1918, and our imagined driver was in command of one of the fifteen vehicles that crashed off the same sharp bend on Highway 73 that day as their drivers fought to escape a terrifying fate. Twenty-five people were killed in motor accidents on that stretch of highway alone. They were running from a death that could have been much worse than the swift and savage mercy of a wreck: death by the flames of the Cloquet Fire.

Starting near a railroad in Sturgeon Lake, Minnesota, the Cloquet Fire began exactly as the Great Hinckley Fire did: a quick railway spark on a pile of dry slash. The resulting firestorm had a brutal swiftness that no one had been expecting. Even though the people of the area had motor cars to flee in, unlike the Peshtigo residents of fifty years before, hundreds of them failed to outrun the pursuing blaze. The firestorm came upon the people of Moose Lake with so much speed that two hundred of them were killed in their homes before they even had a chance to evacuate.

Moose Lake was one of 38 towns and villages that were horribly and hopelessly destroyed in that peaceful country area. Four hundred fifty-three people died, and ten thousand buildings were razed to the ground, with forty of them being schools. The local economy was devastated by the loss of hundreds of thousands of farm animals—part of $100 million in damages.

The Great Lakes area was a hotspot for fires, and it suffered horrifically as a result of these natural disasters. But wherever there is something to burn, there can be firestorms. The rest of the United States was not safe from wildfire.

Nothing is.

* * * *

Ed Pulaski could see that the young man was on the very verge of panic. The strange red light that filled the old mine tunnel reflected in the man's eyes; they were white-edged with fear, startlingly bright in his soot-streaked face. He kept looking back toward the mouth of the tunnel. The flicker of flame was just visible outside, pushing thick wisps of smoke into the tunnel, which collected and lay thick against the low ceiling.

Pulaski had to make several attempts to shout at the youngster, struggling to fill his lungs with air that had turned toxic by the smoke. He told the man to lie down as the rest of his men were doing: face down and trembling in the inadequate little trickle of water that ran down the middle of the tunnel. But the man was too frightened to reason with. He backed away, ready to bolt.

There was nothing else to do. Pulaski knew that if this boy ran, the rest of them could follow, and he hadn't come all this way to save these 45 men only to see them die as the result of the folly of one. Yanking his pistol from its holster, he leveled it at the young man, trying to keep his hoarse and raw voice as serious as he could.

He told the boy to get down or he'd shoot him. And perhaps he meant it: there would be something far more merciful about the crack of the bullet than those heartless flames outside.

Luckily for Pulaski, the threat worked. The young man threw himself down on the floor and stayed there, as did Pulaski and all the other men, while outside, in Pulaski's words, "the whole world seemed to be aflame."

Pulaski couldn't really blame the youngster for being terrified. It was a terrible time to be a firefighter. Starting in late April 1910, Idaho had more or less been on fire for four seemingly endless months.

That fire season had been one of the driest and busiest that Pulaski had ever seen; it was certainly the worst that the fledgling Forest Service had ever seen, but that wasn't saying much, considering it was only five years old. They had just begun to think that the season was finally over when August 20th came. Hurricane-force winds had roared across the state, sending smoldering embers into a roaring wall of fire that devoured everything hapless enough to end up in its path. Firefighters had been out in the woods struggling against those blazes for hours before the Forest Service and the US Army realized that it was to no avail. Pulaski's day had started as a rescue mission: he was sent to retrieve the fire crews and bring them home. There would be no stopping that fire. Everyone needed to be evacuated.

Pulaski had gathered 45 men that day, and then the fire had caught up with them. His knowledge of the trails surrounding Pacer Creek was the only thing that stood between the men and their fiery deaths. Leading them into the old mine tunnel was their only hope. Pulaski kept them there until smoke inhalation choked him into unconsciousness.

When he woke up, it was to one of the men telling the others, "The boss is dead."

Pulaski sat up. "Like hell I am!"

He was very much alive, but five of the men were not so lucky. It was with only forty men that Pulaski emerged into a world that seemed to have perished in the endless blaze. Three million acres had been burned to a crisp in what became known as the Great Fire of 1910, the largest wildfire in American history. Even the US Army had been deployed in a bid to stop the flames, including the famous all-black "Buffalo soldiers" of the 25th Infantry, but it was all to no avail. The fire grew so enormous that its soot was blown all the way to Greenland; smoke from the blaze made people cough and splutter in New England, nearly three thousand miles away.

The loss of life was devastating for the firefighting community. Of the 86 people that died, 78 of those were firefighters. And if it hadn't been for Ed Pulaski's quick thinking, that number would have been considerably higher.

* * * *

Wildfires are not only a part of history. Humanity has tamed, to some extent, many of the evils that have pursued it through the millennia, like smallpox and legalized slavery. But the mighty power of fire still eludes many of mankind's attempts to break its spirit.

Almost a hundred and fifty years have passed since the Great Fire of Peshtigo and the modern day, and countless great improvements have been made in both the prevention of fires and in firefighting. Today, the Great Fire of Peshtigo could perhaps have been prevented if the small fires had been put out early with the help of helicopters slinging huge buckets filled with hundreds of pounds of water. Courageous men and women all around the world are now professionally trained to face these deadly disasters on behalf of their fellow humans. But sometimes, even the best and bravest of people aren't able to stand against the power of Mother Nature herself.

The Camp Fire of 2018 is proof that firestorms remain a phenomenon that mankind can't hope to control. California had never suffered before the blazing power of a firestorm the way that it did just a few years ago.

Starting on November 8th, 2018, along the banks of Camp Creek in California, a fire was whipped up into a mighty firestorm that engulfed 153,000 acres in the northern part of the state. This time, a day or two days would not be enough to bring the fire under control. One thousand firefighters faced the roaring flames, and they did so for more than two weeks, battling against its power for seventeen days straight as more and more of the populous state disappeared into the heartless ravages of the blaze. Eighty-five people died; eighteen thousand homes were consumed by the fire, and the entire town of Paradise was destroyed, just like Sugar Bush had been more than a century ago.

The United States, Canada, Australia, and many other countries all around the globe continue to battle raging wildfires on a regular basis.

In fact, global warming threatens to undo all of the work that fire prevention experts have fought to achieve in the past two centuries. Yet day after day, all around the world, there are heroes who stand between humanity and the might of wildfires. And there always will be.

Conclusion

Wherever disaster goes, heroism follows.
This world will never be completely free of natural disasters. We live in a universe so much bigger than we are, facing forces of nature that we can barely understand, let alone control. One only has to gaze up at even an ordinary thunderstorm to feel how puny we really are and how powerless we are in the face of nature's majestic strength. None of us are capable of halting a volcano in its path, turning aside a meteorite, soothing a tornado, or stopping a tsunami. And even the greatest teams of the most well-trained men and women the world has ever seen can't hope to stand a chance against the twisting, vengeful power of a fire tornado.

It's also true that the whole story of human history is filled with the story of its vice. We have suffered greatly at the hands of Mother Nature, yet we have suffered just as greatly at the hands of each other. People have been killers since the dawn of the human race. Every day, we all face varying degrees of evil and malice, from the burning fury of revenge and cruelty to the simple hatred of petty injustices.

There is something about a natural disaster—something about facing a force greater than all of us—that brings out the true nature of all people, whether that nature is cowardly or courageous, selfish or compassionate. In every blazing fire, there will be someone who runs away and leaves others to perish. In every famine, there will be those who steal from the mouths of others to feed themselves.

Yet there will also always be those who dare to stand up for others, those who will sacrifice themselves for the people they care about, whether they know them well or not. There will always be the pure of heart to rise against the oncoming danger and face it head-on for the sake of their loved ones, and the Great Fire of Peshtigo was no exception.

This book is dedicated to those courageous souls who stand against the destructive power of wildfires. It's for the Ojibwe who came to the aid of Abram Place, honoring him for his courage in marrying the woman he loved despite what society said about their union. It's for Father Pernin who staggered along the riverbanks, pushing stunned people away from their deaths and into the saving waters. It's for Lars Korstad as he poured bucketfuls of water over his wife and child, fighting to save the people who made up his entire world. It's for Amelia Desrochers' mother, stuffing her daughter's little bare feet into her shoes and keeping her cool on the burning barge as others leaped into the river to their deaths. It's for little Joseph LaCrosse who scooped a crying baby into his arms and ran to save her in the face of a wall of flame. It's for William Barry and Edward Best, racing with their train over a burning bridge to save hundreds of lives. It's for Ed Pulaski as he led 45 firefighters into the relative safety of an old mine tunnel. It's for the one thousand firefighters who strove against the Camp Fire, for the 343 firefighters who died in 9/11, and for the men and women all over the world who get up every day to run into burning places when everyone else is running out.

And it's for all those faceless heroes whose exploits have been swallowed up either by history or by fire. This book has explored the lives of the people who lived to tell the tale of the Great Peshtigo Fire, but many of them did not. Many people died trying to save their loved ones, trying to save strangers, and trying to save themselves. We don't even know how many of them there were, for even the records of their existence had been wiped from the world by the might of the blaze.

This is for them. Long may their voices live on.

Sources

The Wisconsin Historical Society: https://www.wisconsinhistory.org/
The Milwaukee Public Museum: http://mpm.edu/
WHS Library-Archives Staff 2009, *Peshtigo, Wisconsin - A Brief History*, Wisconsin Historical Society, viewed 31 March 2020, <https://www.wisconsinhistory.org/Records/Article/CS2491>
Johnson, M. 2015, *Mastodon mystery*, Journal Sentinel, viewed 31 March 2020, <http://archive.jsonline.com/news/wisconsin/researcher-unravels-century--old-wooly-tale-to-find-truth-behind-legendary-massive-bones-b99502786z1-304635421.html/>
Jovaag, S. 2015, *Geologists Rewrite the Story of Wisconsin's Boaz Mastodon*, Wisconsin Live, viewed 31 March 2020, <https://www.wisconsinlife.org/story/geologists-rewrite-the-story-of-wisconsins-boaz-mastodon/>
Savidge, N. 2015, *Newly discovered roots of Boaz mastodon on display at Wisconsin Science Festival*, Wisconsin State Journal, viewed 31 March 2020, <https://madison.com/wsj/news/local/education/university/newly-discovered-roots-of-boaz-mastodon-on-display-at-wisconsin/article_b4447ea7-1f82-5e72-9264-ca2b4f94c864.html>
Wien, T. *Nicolet, Explorations of*, Dictionary of American History, viewed 31 March 2020, <https://www.encyclopedia.com/people/history/us-history-biographies/jean-nicolet>

Gordon, S. 2017, *Wisconsin's Remaining Effigy Mounds are the Tip of a Historical Iceberg*, WisContext, viewed 31 March 2020, <https://www.wiscontext.org/wisconsins-remaining-effigy-mounds-are-tip-historical-iceberg>

Nelson, C. 2018, *The 1871 Peshtigo Fire: How my Great-Great-Great-Grandparents survived the deadliest fire in U. S. history*, Medium, viewed 1 April 2020, <https://medium.com/@chrisnelsonMET/the-1871-peshtigo-fire-how-my-great-great-great-grandparents-survived-the-deadliest-fire-in-u-s-e627efd17d13>

Pernin, P. 1874, *The Great Fire of Peshtigo: An Eyewitness Account*, Wisconsin Electric Reader, viewed March and April 2020, <http://digicoll.library.wisc.edu/WIReader/WER2002-0.html>

The Peshtigo Fire Museum website: http://peshtigofiremuseum.com/

Knickelbine, S. 2012, *The Great Peshtigo Fire: Stories and Science from America's Deadliest Fire*, Wisconsin Historical Society Press

Cayemberg, C. 2011, *Tombstone Tuesday – Eli and Florence Cayemberg*, Have You Seen My Roots?, viewed March and April 2020, <http://haveyouseenmyroots.blogspot.com/2011/01/tombstone-tuesday-eli-and-florence.html>

Cayemberg, C. 2013, *Peshtigo – Recording the Survivors' Tales*, Have You Seen My Roots?, viewed March and April 2020, <http://haveyouseenmyroots.blogspot.com/2011/01/tombstone-tuesday-eli-and-florence.html>

Wells, R. W. 1968, *Fire At Peshtigo*, Internet Archive, viewed March and April 2020, <https://archive.org/stream/FireAtPeshtigo/Fire-At-Peshtigo_djvu.txt>

Kasten, P. 2011, *Tabernacle survives 1871 Peshtigo fire*, Madison Catholic Herald, viewed March and April 2020, <http://madisoncatholicherald.org/news/state/2556-tabernacle-survives-1871-peshtigo-fire.html>

ABC Science 2013, *Fire tornado: how bushfires create their own weather*, ABC Science, viewed 6 April 2020, <https://www.youtube.com/watch?v=rqYEeivt8Eg>

History.com Editors 2019, *Massive fire burns in Wisconsin*, A&E Television Networks, viewed March and April 2020, <https://www.history.com/this-day-in-history/massive-fire-burns-in-wisconsin>

Brown, G. 2017, *A Peshtigo Fire Story of Survival*, Wisconsin Public Radio, viewed March and April 2020, <https://www.wpr.org/peshtigo-fire-story-survival>

Louie, D. 2018, *'Firenado' vs. 'fire whirl' - an expert explains the difference*, viewed 6 April 2020, <https://abc7news.com/butte-county-fire-where-is-the-near-me-today-california-wildfire/4657481/>

Mistrokostas, S. 2019, *The 10 deadliest wildfires in US history*, Business Insider, viewed 6 April 2020, <https://www.businessinsider.com/the-deadliest-wildfires-in-us-history-2019-2?IR=T>

Hagerty, C. 2019, *The Survivors*, Vox, viewed 6 April 2020, <https://www.vox.com/the-highlight/2019/10/16/20908291/camp-fire-wildfire-california-paradise-survivors>

Wootson, C. R. 2018, *The deadliest, most destructive wildfire in California's history has finally been contained*, The Washington Post, viewed 6 April 2020, <https://www.washingtonpost.com/nation/2018/11/25/camp-fire-deadliest-wildfire-californias-history-has-been-contained/>

Larson, D. 2014, *Heritage: The 1894 Hinckley Fire Still Echoes for Families Today*, Lake Superior Magazine, viewed 6 April 2020, <https://www.lakesuperior.com/the-lake/heritage-the-1894-hinckley-fire-still-echoes-for-families-today/>

History.com Editors 2019, *Fire rages in Minnesota*, A&E Television Networks, viewed 6 April 2020, <https://www.history.com/this-day-in-history/fire-rages-in-minnesota>

Anonymous, *Blazing Battles: The 1910 Fire and Its Legacy*, Your National Forests Magazine, viewed 6 April 2020, <https://www.nationalforests.org/our-forests/your-national-forests-magazine/blazing-battles-the-1910-fire-and-its-legacy>

Hart, A. 2015, *Idaho history: The Great Forest Fire of 1910 was Idaho's deadliest*, Idaho Statesman, viewed 6 April 2020, <https://www.idahostatesman.com/news/local/article41567604.html>

Hardy, M. 2015, *1881 Michigan Fire Forever Changed the Thumb*, ThumbWind, viewed 6 April 2020, <https://thumbwind.com/2015/09/11/1881-michigan-fire/>

History.com Editors 2018, *Chicago Fire of 1871*, A&E Television Networks, viewed 6 April 2020, <https://www.history.com/topics/19th-century/great-chicago-fire>

Abbott, K. 2012, *What (or Who) Caused the Great Chicago Fire?*, Smithsonian Magazine, viewed 6 April 2020, <https://www.smithsonianmag.com/history/what-or-who-caused-the-great-chicago-fire-61481977/>

Baalke, R. 2004, *Could a Meteorite or Comet Cause All the Fires of 1871?*, Meteorite-Identification.com, viewed 6 April 2020, <http://meteorite-identification.com/mwnews/08232004.htm>

Goggin, B., and McLaughlin, K. 2018, *A raging wildfire has burned the town of Paradise, California to the ground*, Insider, viewed 6 April 2020, <https://www.insider.com/california-fire-burned-town-of-paradise-california-to-the-ground-2018-11>

Illustrations:

Illustration I:
https://commons.wikimedia.org/wiki/File:Profile_Portrait_of_Pete_Moos-c1913.jpg

Illustration II:
https://commons.wikimedia.org/wiki/File:Peshtigo_Harbor,_Wisconsin,_1871.jpg

Illustration III:
https://commons.wikimedia.org/wiki/File:The_Peshtigo_Fire_showing_people_seeking_refuge_in_the_Peshtigo_River.jpg

Illustration IV:
https://upload.wikimedia.org/wikipedia/commons/6/6d/PeshtigoFireCemetery.jpg

Illustration V:
https://commons.wikimedia.org/wiki/File:Firestorm_Mirror_Plateu.jpg

Here's another book by Captivating History that you might be interested in

www.ingramcontent.com/pod-product-compliance
Lightning Source LLC
LaVergne TN
LVHW041647060526
838200LV00040B/1753